How to *Write* an I.E.P.

Fourth Edition

John I. Arena

Academic Therapy Publications
Novato, California

Editor: Michael Milone, PhD

Academic Therapy Publications
High Noon Books
20 Commercial Boulevard
Novato, California 94949-6191

Books, tests, and materials for and about the learning disabled.

International Standard Book Number: 1-57128-443-5

16 15 14 13 12 11 10 09 08 07
10 09 08 07 06 05 04 03 02 01

Acknowledgements

A word of appreciation is given to reviewers Suzanne Shirley and Nora Thompson.

Special thanks for this 4th Edition is given to Dr. Michael Milone, who went through hundreds of pages of IDEA regulations and presented them in a clear, concise manner, remaining true to the previous editions of this publication.

Jim Arena
Academic Therapy Publications

About the Author

John Arena served the field of special education as editor/publisher of Academic Therapy Publications from 1965 until his untimely death in 1989.

A man of many talents, John was known for his expertise as a reading specialist, college instructor, writer, editor, and publisher. Early in his career as an educator, he taught physically disabled students, and later became principal of a school in Marin County, California. He subsequently served as assistant to the director of the DeWitt Reading Clinic where the journal *Academic Therapy* was begun. Soon after, John and his wife, Anna, founded the Arena School and Learning Center in San Rafael, California. This center served learning disabled students, and the Arenas began their long service to the community.

John Arena was a generous man whose true spirit was concern and caring for others, characteristics that earned him many awards and honors. Among those he received were Honorary Membership in the Optometric Extension Program Foundation, several Awards of Recognition from the Association for Children with Learning Disabilities, and the UNESCO Association award for significant contribution to the field of literacy.

Contents

Foreword

by Suzanne Shirley, Special Education Department Chair
Redwood High School

The majority of students appear to learn at a steady and even pace along with their peers. They enter school, and without much effort, learn well from their teachers. They acquire reading skills with ease and understanding, calculate quickly and well, and write fluidly, learning equally well from either oral or written presentations. These young people also get along well with their peers and understand the social aspects of working well as members of a group.

These are not the students I meet in my special education classroom. My students struggle and need specialized instruction in order to succeed. Working with them can be a challenge; watching them thrive is a real joy.

It has been over thirty years since the first laws were formulated to protect educationally challenged individuals to make it possible for them to progress with their learning. Over the years, those laws have been refined and most recently, significantly changed. As a parent, you will want to be well informed regarding your child's rights. As a teacher, an administrator, or a counselor, you will want to see that each student has a free and appropriate education. This may mean that the I.E.P process is explored for a student and that formalized plans are written.

The latest edition of *How to Write an I.E.P.* is a readable, comprehensive, and sensitive reference book on special needs students. It speaks to all of the people who should be involved in the IEP process. You will be impressed with its completeness, including the depth of research presented. I recommend this book without reservation, knowing that it will be referred to often to clarify your thinking.

Introduction

Thousands of IEPs—Individualized Education Programs—have been written since 1975. In that year, Public Law 94-142, the Education for All Handicapped Children Act, was overwhelmingly passed in Congress, bringing to fruition the persistent and untiring efforts of a group of dedicated parents, educators, and legislators. Since that time, PL 94-142 has been reauthorized several times, most recently in 2004 as the Individuals with Disabilities Education Act.

In the years before PL 94-142, children and adults with disabilities had limited options in education. Too many were institutionalized, and for those who lived at home, educational opportunities were highly restricted. In many cases, disabled children or adults were misdiagnosed, particularly those who did not seem to learn by traditional methods. They fell into no existing category of exceptionality. Scores of bright, eager youngsters were falling by the wayside, and their teachers and parents were baffled and frustrated. Eventually, this pattern of learning problems was given a name—learning disabilities—and it was included in the groundbreaking law.

PL 94-142 included several novel elements. Among them are a free, appropriate public education (FAPE), education in the least restrictive environment (LRE), and a written document prepared for each child receiving special education services, the individualized education program (IEP). It is the latter element on which this book focuses because the IEP process has become a way of life in American public schools.

If the preparation of an IEP were no more than placing a pencil to paper, then *How to Write an I.E.P.* would not be necessary. The law, however, is both extensive and specific, not only in detailing the requirements of an IEP, but also in defining its relationship with the many other facets of the child's total educational program.

The central concept in preparing this handbook was that teachers (both special and regular education), diagnosticians, administrators, parents, and others involved in IEP preparation and implementation, would profit from a brief, easy-to-use guide. It is meant to serve as a reference for making sure that all factors of consequence are given the consideration they require.

Throughout this guide, stated or implied, is a focus on both the intent and spirit of the law. One important consideration is the role of the family in participating in IEP preparation; another is the child-centered orientation. The teacher and other members of the team are required to state accurately and objectively what the child can do, the child's needs, and the ways they will be met. Yet in dealing with quantifications, there is always a danger that human, social, emotional, and affective needs may be minimized or set aside. Programming and planning demand a level of concern that surpasses scores on an assessment; a concern for the individuality and uniqueness of the student is imperative.

Finally, the IEP is exactly what it says. It is a mandated program, not a legal contract. The IEP should always be open to modification by means of group interaction involving the family, the student where appropriate, and the public school staff in an effort to provide the student with the most appropriate education.

Preface

Where Parents Can Find More Help

by Nora Thompson, Executive Director
Matrix Parent Network and Resource Center

All parents have hopes and dreams for their children, and they want to the do the best job they can to ensure that their children have many chances to be happy and successful. When the child is identified as "different," the family may feel unprepared for what lies ahead. That is why a book like *How to Write an I.E.P.* is so important. It offers families and educators concrete information about special education and the Individualized Education Program, both of which may be confusing. As a parent of a child with unique needs, I have always been on a quest for strategies and information sources that would help me make sense of what all the professionals were talking about and give me some confidence that I was making the right decisions for my daughter's future.

As you can see from this book, there are many factors to consider, and all the pieces of the puzzle must fit together in order for the child to benefit from his or her education. A critical question is "Where else can parents get more information they might need in order to make sense of this complex process and truly become equal partners in the IEP team?" Besides the extensive resources listed in the back of this book, there are some additional places that parents may want to explore. Through these resources, families may seek more in-depth information pertaining to their child. They may also explore their state's way of implementing special education services or learn specifics about the impact of their child's diagnosis.

It is important to consider why parents would need more information. Can parents figure it all out the first time they attend an IEP meeting? Probably not. Will it take some time and energy for the pieces to make sense and start to fall into place? Probably. Are there places to go, resources to look at, and people to help families become familiar with all of this? Fortunately, there are many places for parents to learn more about the process.

Parents often believe that they have little of value to share about their child. They might feel the educational professionals are far more skilled and knowledgeable about how children with special needs learn best. "What do I know, I am just a parent" is a very common feeling parents have when dealing with the professional members of the IEP team. Parents, however, are the constant in a child's life. They can share a wealth of information and knowledge about an individual child, even if they don't have the all the terminology that the other members of the team may have. Ideally, the educational professionals will work closely with parents to incorporate the important information that families can contribute about their child. Information such as likes, dislikes, hobbies, and so on can contribute significantly to creating a quality educational program. As parents learn more about the process, their confidence increases as they see how crucial their role is.

Parent Resources

Parents have access to many sources of useful information about the education of their children. Among the most important are the Parent Training and Information Centers (PTIs) and Community Parent Resource Centers (CPRCs) in each state. They provide training and information to parents of infants, toddlers, children, and youth with disabilities and to professionals who work with them. This assistance helps parents collaborate more effectively with professionals in meeting the educational needs of children and youth with disabilities. The parent centers work to improve educational outcomes for children and youth with all disabilities— emotional, learning, mental, and physical.

There are approximately 100 parent centers in the United States. Staff members in these centers are likely to be parents of children with disabilities or have disabilities themselves. PTIs and CPRCs have developed training and information materials in a variety of formats and languages that will help families become familiar with the IEP process. The centers may also have staff or volunteers who work directly with families, helping them organize their questions and concerns. These parent centers also work with families on effective communication skills, parent professional collaboration, and alternative dispute methods. The primary role of the PTIs/CPRCs is to assist families in becoming informed, confident, and competent so they can function as equal partners in the education process of their children.

The PTIs and CPRCs are listed by state on the website maintained by the Technical Assistance Alliance for Parent Centers: http://www.taalliance.org/. As an option, you may call toll free 888-248-0822 for a listing of your nearest parent center.

Parent-to-parent organizations focus on matching parents with children who may have similar diagnoses or needs. These may be know by a variety of names such Mentor Parents, Visiting Parents, Parent Partners, Buddies, Pals, Advocates, Pilot Parents, Support Parents, and many other such names across America and around the world.

The organizations include experienced parents, often called "veterans," who provide support to other parents whose children have similar special needs or are experiencing a difficult situation. These situations could be the birth of a child with a disability, a parent going through divorce, or a child having problems in school. Mentors or peer counselors share their experiences and help provide resources and referrals to other families. They are the key elements in a parent-to-parent program.

The Beach Center on Disability at the University of Kansas maintains a list of all parent-to-parent organizations on their website:
http://www.beachcenter.org/groups/default.asp?act=p_to_p

Beach Center on Disability
University of Kansas
Haworth Hall
1200 Sunnyside Ave., Room 3136
Lawrence, KS 66045-7534
phone 785-864-7600

National disability groups such as United Cerebral Palsy, National Association of Parents of Visually Impaired, Children, Adults with Attention Deficit Disorders, and Learning Disabilities Association, etc., may have regional or local contacts. These disability-specific groups often have information on useful educational strategies and techniques for children whose learning is impacted because of a disability. Your local parent center will have contact information for groups near you.

Each state department of education often has useful resources to families. These resources can be found by checking your state department of education's Web site. If you don't have access to a computer, you can gain access to one and receive assistance at a local library, school, or university. You may also find it helpful to contact a local elected state representative or senator.

Dispute Resolution

Occasionally, issues arise in the IEP process that cannot be resolved through a regular meeting. There are several options available for parents and schools to resolve these disputes before more formal channels such as due process, the term that describes legal proceedings. It is always best to attempt to solve problems as close to the source as possible. When communicating with the IEP team, families will be more successful when they focus on what's working, stay calm, listen carefully, ask clarifying questions, and look at ways to work collaboratively to meet the child's needs.

If the issue can't be resolved with the IEP team, then parents can go to the site principal or the person in charge of special education services at that school. The communication should be positive and collaborative.

Occasionally, issues can't be resolved at the school level. When this occurs, families can proceed through slightly more formal conflict resolution channels such as a facilitated IEP meeting. This is a voluntary process in which an impartial facilitator conducts the meeting. This facilitator can use helpful strategies that create an environment in which team members work together, listen to one another, and understand each other's viewpoint in an effort to reach agreement.

Alternative dispute resolution (ADR) is a form of mediation where a neutral person works with both parties to resolve disagreements. The resulting written agreement is not binding but shows the commitment of both parties to reach a resolution that is acceptable. In short, it is a win-win situation. More formal still is state mediation where the Office of Administrative Hearings assigns a mediator to help facilitate an agreement.

All of these steps—using good communication, attempting to resolve conflict at the lowest possible level, and engaging in more formal mechanisms such as a facilitated IEP, ADR and state mediation—are options that families may want to explore. Each of these methods provide opportunities to maintain positive ongoing relationships between the families and the educators.

The most formal mechanism, due process, can resolve disagreements, but it is the option of last resort. This process usually involves court proceedings and attorneys, both of which can feel adversarial to the parties involved. It is always the hope that disagreements can be resolved before it is felt necessary to implement due process.

I

The New Law

The tenets of the Individuals with Disabilities Education Act (IDEA), formerly PL94-142, have affected virtually every public school in the United States. The changes required by the law did not take place all at once, but were phased in gradually.

The first phase began in 1977 and required every state to locate all disabled students in need of special services; to submit to the federal government a state plan for the education of disabled students; to develop an individualized education program (IEP) for every student currently enrolled in a public school special education program; and to protect the rights of every disabled student by assuring due process, confidentiality of records, and parental involvement in the IEP process.

In phase two, which started September 1, 1978, the law required a free and appropriate public school education to be available for every disabled child between age 3 and 18; each state must have submitted a revised state plan yearly; an IEP must be written for every disabled child in the state.

In the 1980 phase, the law required that a free, appropriate public education be available to every disabled child from age 3 to 21 (meaning through the twenty-first year).

The law provides four basic educational rights for disabled children:

1. A thorough assessment of the nature and degree of specific disability, in a non-discriminatory manner, and with no single measurement being the sole criterion for evaluation

2. The overall right to a free education appropriately tailored to the needs of each child

3. Placement in the "least restrictive environment" with maximum emphasis on placement of the disabled child with non-disabled children whenever possible (mainstreaming)

4. The provision of supplementary aids and services to help ensure the success of the program

In order to ensure these rights, two procedural safeguards were established in the law: the individualized education program (IEP) and due process procedures for parents.

New Provisions in IDEA 2004

Alignment with No Child Left Behind

The new IDEA refers frequently to No Child Left Behind (NCLB), including the use of IDEA funds for NCLB activities. Parents especially should be aware of the association between IDEA and NCLB. One of the critical requirements for aligning IDEA with NCLB is that special education teachers must meet the highly qualified standard by being certified in special education. New special education teachers who have multiple subjects must meet the NCLB highly qualified standard in at least one core subject area (language arts, math, or science) and will demonstrate competence in other core subject areas. Further, children with disabilities must be included in the assessment system required under the No Child Left Behind Act and schools must report their results through NCLB's adequate yearly progress structure. The IEP team determines how the child with a disability is assessed.

Annual Goals

The child's IEP must contain measurable annual goals and a description of how progress toward meeting those goals will be measured and reported. It is no longer necessary to establish benchmarks and short-term objectives. Special education and related services must be based on peer-reviewed research whenever possible. When appropriate, postsecondary goals and transition services must be included in the IEP beginning when the child is 16. When services are terminated, the school must provide a summary of a child's academic achievement and functional performance, including a recommendation about meeting the child's postsecondary goals.

Child Find

States will establish a policy that describes how appropriate early intervention services are available to all infants and toddlers with disabilities, including those who are homeless or wards of the state. Parents of premature infants or infants with other risk factors associated with learning problems will be informed of the availability of services.

Complaints

Under IDEA 2004, a complaint may be filed relating to the identification, evaluation, educational placement of the child, or the provision of a free appropriate public education to such a child. The complaint is limited to a violation that occurred not more than two years before the date the parent or school district knew or should have known about the alleged action.

Consent for Services

Parental consent must be obtained by a school before providing a child with special education and related services. If consent is not granted, the district may not use procedures such as mediation and due process to provide services.

Determination of Eligibility

Upon completion of the administration of tests and other evaluation materials, a group of qualified professionals and the parents of the child must determine whether the child is a child with a disability. The public agency must provide a copy of the evaluation report and the documentation of the determination of eligibility to the parent.

Dispute Resolution

Mediation will be allowed before filing for a hearing. A "Preliminary Meeting" can be used to seek a resolution before a due process hearing is initiated. The provisions for awarding attorneys' fees have been modified.

Early Childhood Transition

Policies and procedures are to be established to ensure a smooth transition for toddlers receiving early intervention services to exit the service or to enter preschool, school, or other appropriate services.

Early Intervention Services

Because it is so important to identify infants and toddlers with disabilities and provide them with appropriate development opportunities, the new IDEA provides for early intervention services. These services ensure that educators and parents have the necessary tools to improve educational results for children with disabilities.

Evaluation

In conducting the evaluation, a variety of assessment tools and strategies should be used to gather relevant functional, developmental, and academic information, including information provided by the parent. The goals of the evaluation are to determine if the child has a disability and develop the IEP. No single measure may be used, instruments should be technically sound, and they should not discriminate on the basis of race or culture. Once parental consent has been received for evaluation, it must be undertaken within 60 days. Exceptions are children moving between school districts or parents' refusal to make the child available for evaluation.

IEP Team Attendance

Attendance at IEP team meetings is no longer mandatory. A member of the team may be excused from attending if the parent and school district agree that attendance is not necessary, typically because the member's contribution is not being discussed or the member has submitted input in writing. An IEP can be changed without convening the team if the school district and parent agree.

Individualized Family Service Plan (IFSP)

An Individualized Family Service Plan will be developed by family members and service providers to document and guide the early intervention process for children with disabilities and their families. The IFSP should contain information about the services needed to foster a child's development and how the family can facilitate the child's development.

Manifestation Determination

If a student violates a school's code of conduct, the new IDEA allows school personnel to make decisions regarding a change in placement on a case-by-case basis. The provisions to conduct a manifestation determination and to continue educational services in alternative settings have been modified somewhat.

Paperwork Reduction

Fifteen states will carry out pilot programs to reduce paperwork requirements. Up to 15 states can take part in another pilot program to develop comprehensive, multi-year IEPs, not to exceed three years.

Preventing Over-identification

Funds are provided to train school personnel to use instructional strategies and behavioral interventions to prevent over-identification of students with learning disabilities. There will be a special focus on avoiding over-identification of minority students.

School Transfer

When a student with an IEP transfers into a new school, the new school must take steps to promptly obtain the child's records and the previous school must promptly respond. Comparable services must be provided in the new school.

Specific Learning Disabilities

It is no longer necessary to show a severe discrepancy between achievement and intellectual ability in order for a child to be identified as having a specific learning disability. A process known as "response to intervention" with scientific, research-based procedures may be used as a part of the evaluation procedures.

Technology

The development and use of technology is emphasized, including assistive technology devices and services. Technology use is expanded in the IEP process and in the classroom in order to maximize accessibility for children with disabilities, and universal design will make the general education curriculum more available.

How to Obtain a Copy of the IDEA Regulations

The regulations can be downloaded from a number of sources, including the Education Department's website:

http://www.ed.gov/policy/speced/guid/idea/idea2004.html

It is important that teachers, administrators, parents, and diagnosticians become familiar with the master plan for special education in their own state for specific elements. The material in this book is taken from the federal law from which states have drawn up their own master plans. A copy of the law in each state can be obtained from the state website, state legislature representatives, or from your state department of special education at the state capital.

II

IDEA 2004 and the IEP

This is one in a series of documents on IDEA 2004 that have been prepared by the Office of Special Education and Rehabilitative Services (OSERS) in the U.S. Department of Education. This document addresses only the changes to IDEA provisions regarding the content of Individualized Education Programs (IEPs).

The reauthorized *Individuals with Disabilities Education Act* (IDEA) was signed into law on Dec. 3, 2004, by President George W. Bush. The provisions of the act became effective on July 1, 2005, with the exception of some of the elements pertaining to the definition of a "highly qualified teacher" that took effect upon the signing of the act. This is one in a series of documents, prepared by the Office of Special Education and Rehabilitative Services (OSERS) in the U.S. Department of Education, that covers a variety of high-interest topics and brings together the statutory language related to those topics to support constituents in preparing to implement the new requirements. This document addresses only the changes to the provisions of IDEA regarding the content of individualized education programs (IEPs) that took effect on July 1, 2005.

1. Provisions regarding present levels of educational performance, short-term objectives or benchmarks, and annual goals

The IEP must include:

A statement of the child's present levels of academic achievement and functional performance; including, for children who take alternate assessments aligned to

21

alternate achievement standards, a description of benchmarks or short-term objectives; and

A statement of measurable annual goals, including both academic and functional goals. [614(d)(1)(A)(i)(I)-(II)]

2. Provisions regarding assessments

The IEP must include a statement of any individual appropriate accommodations that are necessary to measure the academic achievement and functional performance of the child on state and districtwide assessments consistent with Section 612(a)(16)(A). [614(d)(1)(A)(i)(VI)(aa)]

If the IEP team determines that the child shall take an alternate assessment on a particular state or districtwide assessment of student achievement, the IEP must include a statement of why the child cannot participate in the regular assessment and why the particular alternate assessment selected is appropriate for the child. [614(d)(1)(A)(i)(VI)(bb)]

3. Requirements for measuring progress and reporting progress to parents

The IEP must include a description of:

How the child's progress toward meeting the annual goals will be measured; and

When periodic reports on the progress the child is making toward meeting the annual goals (such as through the use of quarterly or other periodic reports, concurrent with the issuance of report cards) will be provided.
[614(d)(1)(A)(i)(III)]

4. Provisions regarding the statement of services

The IEP must include a statement of the special education and related services and supplementary aids and services, based on peer-reviewed research to the extent practicable, to be provided to the child or on behalf of the child, and a statement of the program modifications or supports for school personnel that will be provided for the child. [614(d)(1)(A)(i)(IV)]

5. Secondary transition requirements

Beginning not later than the first IEP to be in effect when the child is 16, and updated annually thereafter, (note: eliminates age 14 requirements) the IEP must include:

Appropriate measurable postsecondary goals based upon age-appropriate transition assessments related to training, education, employment and, where appropriate, independent living skills; and

The transition services (including courses of study) needed to assist the child in reaching those goals. [614(d)(1)(A)(i)(VIII)]

6. Requirements for children with disabilities transferring school districts within a state and between states

Within-state transfers: In the case of a child with a disability who transfers school districts within the same academic year, who enrolls in a new school, and who had an IEP that was in effect in the same state, the local education agency (LEA) shall provide such child with a free appropriate public education (FAPE), including services comparable to those described in the previously held IEP, in consultation with the parents, until such time as the LEA adopts the previously held IEP or develops, adopts, and implements a new IEP that is consistent with federal and state law. [614(d)(2)(C)(i)(I)]

Between-state transfers: In the case of a child with a disability who transfers school districts within the same academic year, who enrolls in a new school, and who had an IEP that was in effect in another state, the new LEA must provide such child with FAPE, including services comparable to those described in the previously held IEP, in consultation with the parents, until such time as the LEA conducts an evaluation pursuant to IDEA requirements at Section 614(a)(1), if determined to be necessary by such agency, and develops a new IEP, if appropriate, that is consistent with federal and state law. [614(d)(2)(C)(i)(II)]

Transmittal of records: To facilitate the transition for a child described above, the new school in which the child enrolls shall take reasonable steps to promptly obtain the child's records, including the IEP and supporting documents and any other records relating to the provision of special education or related services to the child, from the previous school in which the child was enrolled, pursuant to 34 CFR Section 99.31(a)(2); and the previous school in which the child was enrolled shall take reasonable steps to promptly respond to such request from the new school. [614(d)(2)(C)(ii)]

7. New rule of construction

Nothing in Section 614 shall be construed to require: (1) that additional information be included in a child's IEP beyond what is explicitly required in Section 614; or (2) the IEP team to include information under one component of a child's IEP that is already contained under another component of such IEP. [614(d)(1)(A)(ii)]

III

Definitions

1. **Special Education** Specially designed instruction, at no cost to the parents or guardians, to meet the unique needs of a disabled child, including classroom instruction, instruction in physical education, home instruction, and instruction in hospitals and institutions.

2. **Child with a Disability** A child with mental retardation, hearing impairment (including deafness), speech or language impairment, visual impairment (including blindness), serious emotional disturbance (referred to in this title as 'emotional disturbance'), orthopedic impairment, autism, traumatic brain injury, other health impairment, or specific learning disability; and who, by reason thereof, needs special education and related services.

3. **Related Services** Transportation, and such developmental, corrective, and other supportive services (including speech-language pathology and audiology services, interpreting services, psychological services, physical and occupational therapy, recreation, including therapeutic recreation, social work services, school nurse services designed to enable a child with a disability to receive a free appropriate public education as described in the individualized education program of the child, counseling services, including rehabilitation counseling, orientation and mobility services, and medical services, except that such medical services shall be for diagnostic and evaluation purposes only) as may be required to assist a child with a disability to benefit from special education, and includes the early identification and assessment of disabling conditions in children.

4. **Free Appropriate Public Education (FAPE)** Special education and related services that have been provided at public expense, under public supervision and direction, and without charge that meet the standards of the state educational agency and include an appropriate preschool, elementary school, or secondary school education in the state and are provided in conformity with the individualized education program required under section.

5. **Least Restrictive Environment (LRE)** To the maximum extent appropriate, children with disabilities, including children in public or private institutions or other care facilities, are educated with children who are not disabled, and special classes, separate schooling, or other removal of children with disabilities from the regular educational environment occurs only when the nature or severity of the disability of a child is such that education in regular classes with the use of supplementary aids and services cannot be achieved satisfactorily.

6. **Parent** A natural, adoptive, or foster parent of a child (unless a foster parent is prohibited by state law from serving as a parent), a guardian (but not the state if the child is a ward of the state), an individual acting in the place of a natural or adoptive parent (including a grandparent, stepparent, or other relative) with whom the child lives, or an individual who is legally responsible for the child's welfare; or an individual assigned to be a surrogate parent.

7. **Native Language** The language normally used by the individual or, in the case of a child, the language normally used by the parents of the child.

8. **Highly Qualified Teacher** The teacher has obtained full state certification as a special education teacher (including certification obtained through alternative routes to certification), or passed the state special education teacher licensing examination, and holds a license to teach in the state as a special education teacher, except that when used

with respect to a teacher in a public charter school, the term means that the teacher meets the requirements set forth in the state's public charter school law.

9. **Local Educational Agency (LEA)** A public board of education or other public authority legally constituted within a state for either administrative control or direction of, or to perform a service function for, public elementary schools or secondary schools in a city, county, township, school district, or other political subdivision of a state, or for such combination of school districts or counties as are recognized in a state as an administrative agency for its public elementary schools or secondary schools.

10. **State Educational Agency (SEA)** The state board of education or other agency or officer primarily responsible for the state supervision of public elementary schools and secondary schools, or, if there is no such officer or agency, an officer or agency designated by the Governor or by state law.

11. **Educational Service Agency** A regional public multiservice agency authorized by state law to develop, manage, and provide services or programs to local educational agencies; and recognized as an administrative agency for purposes of the provision of special education and related services provided within public elementary schools and secondary schools of the state; and includes any other public institution or agency having administrative control and direction over a public elementary school or secondary school.

12. **Public Agency** The SEA, LEAs, ESAs, or public charter schools that are not otherwise included as LEAs or ESAs and any other political subdivisions of the state that are responsible for providing education services to children with disabities.

IV

Related Services—What Are They?

According to IDEA, children with disabilities are those in need of special education and related services. In an earlier section, the term "related services" was briefly defined, but because these services are so critical to meeting the needs of disabled learners and the formulation of an IEP, related services are explained more thoroughly in this section.

The law describes related services as "transportation, and such developmental, corrective, and other supportive services (including speech-language pathology and audiology services, interpreting services, psychological services, physical and occupational therapy, recreation, including therapeutic recreation, social work services, school nurse services designed to enable a child with a disability to receive a free appropriate public education as described in the individualized education program of the child, counseling services, including rehabilitation counseling, orientation and mobility services, and medical services, except that such medical services shall be for diagnostic and evaluation purposes only) as may be required to assist a child with a disability to benefit from special education, and includes the early identification and assessment of disabling conditions in children." Not included are medical devices that are surgically implanted, the optimization device functioning, maintenance of the device, or the replacement of a device.

1. **Audiology** includes the identification of children with hearing loss and the determination of the range, nature, and degree of the loss. Also included is a referral for medical or other professional attention for the habilitation of

hearing, providing services such as language habilitation, auditory training, speech reading (lip-reading), hearing evaluation, and speech conservation. The law also supports creation and administration of programs for preventing hearing loss, counseling and guidance of children, parents, and teachers about hearing loss, and the determination of the child's needs for group and individual amplification, selecting and fitting an appropriate aid, and evaluating the effectiveness of amplification.

2. **Counseling Services** refers to services provided by qualified social workers, psychologists, guidance counselors, or other qualified personnel.

3. **Early Identification** refers to the implementation of a formal plan for identifying a disability as early as possible in a child's life.

4 **Interpreting Services**, as used with respect to children who are deaf or hard of hearing, includes oral transliteration services, cued language transliteration services, and Sign Language interpreting services.

5. **Medical Services** means services provided by a licensed physician to determine a child's medically related disability that results in the child's need for special education and related services.

6. **Occupational Therapy** describes services provided by a qualified occupational therapist. It includes improving, developing, or restoring functions impaired or lost through illness, injury, or deprivation. It also covers improving the ability to perform tasks for independent functioning when these functions are impaired or lost and preventing, through early intervention, initial or further impairment or loss of function.

7. **Orientation and Mobility Services** are provided to blind

or visually impaired students by qualified personnel to enable those students to attain systematic orientation and safe movement within their environments in school, home, and community. Also included is travel instruction such as understanding spatial and environmental concepts, using a long cane or service animal, employing remaining vision and distance low vision aids, and other concepts, techniques, and tools.

8. **Parent Counseling and Training** means assisting parents in understanding the special needs of their child, providing parents with information about child development, and helping parents acquire the necessary skills that will allow them to support the implementation of their child's IEP or IFSP.

9. **Physical Therapy** means services provided by a qualified physical therapist.

10. **Psychological Services** include administering psychological and educational tests and other assessment procedures, as well as interpreting the results. Such services also consist of obtaining, integrating and interpreting information about child behavior and conditions relating to learning; consulting with other staff members in planning the school program to meet the special educational needs of children as indicated by psychological tests, interviews, direct observation, and behavioral evaluations. The law provides for planning and managing a program of psychological services; including psychological counseling for children and parents, and assisting in developing positive behavioral intervention strategies.

11. **Recreation** includes assessment of leisure function, therapeutic recreation services, recreation programs in schools and community agencies, and leisure education.

12. **Rehabilitation Counseling Services** means services

provided by qualified personnel in individual or group sessions that focus specifically on career development, employment preparation, achieving independence, and integration in the workplace and community. The term also refers to vocational rehabilitation programs funded under the Rehabilitation Act of 1973.

13. **School Nurse Services** refer to services provided by a qualified school nurse to enable a child with a disability to receive FAPE as described in the child's IEP.

14. **Social Work Services** include preparing a social or developmental history on a child with a disability and offering group and individual counseling with the child and family. The term also refers to working with parents or others on those problems in a child's living situation (home, school, and community) that affect the child's adjustment in school. Also included are mobilizing school and community resources to enable the child to learn as effectively as possible in his or her educational program and providing assistance in developing positive behavioral intervention strategies.

15. **Speech-Language Pathology** services refer to the identification of children with speech or language impairments and diagnosis and appraisal of the impairments. Also included are referral for medical or other professional attention necessary for the habilitation of speech or language impairments and provision of these services for habilitation or prevention. Counseling and guidance of parents, children, and teachers regarding the nature of these disorders are covered by the law.

16. **Transportation** includes travel to and from school as well as between schools. It also refers to travel in and around school buildings and specialized equipment such as adapted buses, lifts, and so on that may be required to provide

special transportation for a child with a disability.

Under IDEA, each public agency must take steps to provide nonacademic and extracurricular services and activities so that children with disabilities are afforded an equal opportunity for participation in such services and activities. This includes counseling services, athletics, transportation, health services, recreational activities, special interest groups or clubs sponsored by the public agency, referrals to agencies that provide assistance to individuals with disabilities, and employment of students, including both employment by the public agency and assistance in making outside employment available.

Physical education services, specially designed if necessary, must be made available. The child with a disability must be afforded opportunity to participate in the regular physical education program available to nondisabled children, unless that child is enrolled full time in a separate facility or the child needs specially designed physical education as prescribed in the IEP. The public agency responsible for the child's education must provide specially designed physical education, if it is prescribed in the IEP, or make arrangements for those services to be provided by another public or private program. If the child is enrolled in a separate facility, the public agency responsible for the education of a child is also responsible for ensuring that the child receives appropriate physical education services.

In addition, the law further states that each public agency shall take steps to ensure that its children with disabilities have available to them the variety of educational programs and services available to nondisabled children in the area served by the agency, including art, music, industrial arts, consumer and homemaking education, and vocational education.

All related services must be provided without any charge

to the parent. In most cases, the local school district is responsible for providing the related services directly or by contracting with appropriate persons. In some states, related services, including occupational and physical therapy and mental health services, are provided by other state agencies. However, if the other agency does not provide the service, and it can be successfully demonstrated to the IEP team or to a due process hearing officer that the services are necessary for the student to benefit from education, the school district is responsible for providing them. Disputes regarding related services are resolved through the fair hearing procedures in the same fashion as disputes about any other part of the child's special education program.

The local education agency is not usually required to pay for the cost of special education and related services if a child with a disability attends a private school. The exception is when the parents enroll the child in a private school and the court or hearing officer finds that the agency had not made a free appropriate public education available in a timely manner prior to that enrollment and the private placement is appropriate.

V

The Individualized Education Program (IEP)

The four stages of the IEP—development, implementation, review, and revision—are the result of a process. Simply stated, the IEP tells where the child is, where the child should be going, how the child will get there, how long it will take, and how you will know the child has arrived.

The IEP is not a legal contract. It is formulated as a team effort, based on what the child needs—not what the school district (local educational agency) can provide. What the local district cannot provide must be obtained or contracted for.

The IEP team is a group that comprises, in the least, the following individuals:

- the parents of a child with a disability

- not less than one regular education teacher (if the child is or may participate in the regular education environment)

- not less than one special education teacher or special education provider

- a representative of the local educational agency who is qualified to provide or supervise the provision of specially designed instruction and knowledgeable about the special education curriculum and resources

- an individual who can interpret the instructional implications of evaluation results

- at the discretion of the parent or agency, other knowledgeable individuals or related services personnel

- when appropriate, the child with a disability

The IEP, according to the law, is a written statement prepared for each child with a disability and includes the following information:

- the child's present levels of academic achievement and functional performance

- how the disability affects the child's involvement and progress in the general education curriculum, or in the case of preschool children, how the disability affects participation in appropriate activities

- a statement of measurable annual goals, both academic and functional, that enable the child to be involved in and progress through the general education curriculum as well as meet the child's other needs arising from the disability

- a description of benchmarks or short-term objectives for children who take alternate assessments

- a description of how progress toward annual goals will be measured and when progress reports will be provided

- a statement of the special education, related services, and supplementary aids and services to be provided (based on peer-reviewed research to the extent practicable)

- a statement of the modifications or support for school personnel that will be provided for the child to attain the annual goals, be involved in and progress in the general education curriculum, participate in extracurricular and other nonacademic activities, and be educated with other children with and without disabilities

- an explanation of why and to what extent the child will not participate with nondisabled children in the regular class

- a statement of appropriate accommodations needed to measure the academic achievement and functional performance of the child with a disability on state and districtwide assessments

- for children with a disability who take an alternate assessment, a statement of why they cannot participate in the regular assessment and which alternate assessment is appropriate

- the projected date for the beginning of the services and modifications, their frequency, location, and duration

- in the first IEP when the child is 16, appropriate, measurable postsecondary goals based on age-appropriate transition assessments related to training, education, employment, and independent living skills, where appropriate, and the transition services needed to reach the goals

- for children within one year of reaching majority under state law, an indication that the child has been informed of the rights, if any, that will transfer to the child on reaching the age of majority

There is no national form the written statement of the IEP must take. This decision is left to the local education agency, and sample IEP forms are available through the internet sites of state education departments. On the following two pages is an outline of the information found on a typical IEP form. The information was drawn from a review of IEP forms from a sample of states around the country. The order of the information is not critical, nor is the format of the IEP document. Check boxes are used in many state provided forms in order to facilitate the recording of information that can be categorized readily such as type of disability or general areas of instructional need.

- Student and parent information

Primary area of eligibility and secondary, if appropriate

- Special factors
    Behavior
    Limited English proficiency
    Blind or visually impaired
    Deaf or hearing impaired
    Communication needs
    Behaviors that may impede learning or disrupt others
    Assistive technology

- Future considerations (post-secondary education, employment, community participation, recreation and leisure activities, post-secondary opportunities)

- Graduation requirements

- Dates of most recent and next evaluations

- Areas of need

- Strengths and weaknesses: academic, social, life skills, independent daily living

- Present levels of educational and functional performance
    Sources of information

- Medical and health information

- Mobility and transportation considerations
    Emergency evacuation needs, if any

- Adaptive physical education

- Summary of services: education, related services, supplementary services
    Dates, frequency, duration, location, provider

Behavioral interventions, if needed

- Instructional accommodations or modifications (grading, text or notes, lectures, seating options, classroom-based testing, assignments, reinforcement, pacing, specialized materials, other adaptations)

- Transition services

- IEP progress documentation

- Annual goals, benchmarks, and short-term objectives
  How progress will be measured

- Least restrictive environment
  Continuum of placement options
  Supplementary aids, services, modifications, accommodations

- Alternate placements, including private or residential school, preschool, hospital

- Means of informing parents of relevant information such as placement, goals, and progress

- Testing status (participation in state or local assessments) and necessary accommodations or alternate assessment

- Extended school year status, if necessary

- IEP team members and positions and other participants
  Agreement to IEP changes without meeting

- Prior written notice of proposed actions

- Transfer of rights for students approaching majority

- Procedural safeguards notice

VI

How Does the IEP Work?

An IEP must be developed for every child with a disability who is currently receiving or who will receive special education services. The IEP must be in effect before the child receives special education and/or related services. A request for an initial evaluation to determine a disability can be made by a parent, the state education agency, or the local education agency.

The evaluation on which the IEP is based must be undertaken within 60 days of receiving parental consent for the evaluation. An exception is made in the case of a child who changes school districts or whose parents refuse to make the child available for evaluation.

The LEA (Local Educational Agency) must inform the parents of any anticipated evaluation. If a parent refuses to provide consent or fails to respond to a request for an initial evaluation, the LEA may pursue the initial evaluation. If the child is found to have a disability, the LEA is not obligated to provide services without parental consent, nor must an IEP meeting be convened. If the parents cannot be located, the LEA may proceed without their consent.

A new evaluation of a disabled child may be undertaken if the parents or the child's teacher request it. The same is true if the child's academic achievement or functional performance changes in a meaningful way.

Once an evaluation has taken place, a team of qualified professionals and the parent will determine if the child has a disability. The determination should not be made if the child's performance is the result of a lack of appropriate instruction in reading or mathematics, or if the performance reflects limited English proficiency.

During initial and subsequent evaluations, the IEP team and other involved professionals will review a broad range of information, including current classroom-based, local, and state assessments, as well as observations in the classroom and other settings. From these data sources, a determination is made as to whether the child has a disability, what educational needs the child requires, the academic and developmental needs of the child, and what related services are necessary.

The law requires that parents must be notified if the child has a disability and the reasons for this determination. At that point, if the parents consent, the team will meet to create the IEP. Then parents are contacted to set a mutually agreed upon time and place for a conference in which a decision about services will be made. This conference will include those who conducted the assessment, representatives of the school district, the student's teacher (regular and/or special), parent or parents/guardians, and, when appropriate, the student. If parents disagree with the assessment summary or the proposed special service recommendation, they are to be informed of their rights to appeal the decision. After receiving parental consent, special education services can be provided. Again, it is important to remember the native language of the parents must be used in communications, and that all communications should be recorded, including telephone calls.

The child with a disability who changes school districts during the academic year must receive comparable services in the new school as were described in the IEP that was in effect in the old school. The parents should be consulted about the services in the new district, and the services should conform with the requirements of the law. If the transfer takes place into a new state, the LEA must provide comparable services, undertake a new evaluation, and develop a new IEP. In all cases, the new school must take reasonable steps to obtain the disabled child's records, including the IEP and supporting documentation. The previous school must respond promptly to the information request.

The Individualized Family Service Plan (IFSP)

The Individualized Family Service Plan (IFSP) is one of the requirements of IDEA. The IFSP is meant to describe and record the early intervention activities for children with disabilities and the needs of their families. The IFSP contains information about the services necessary to promote a child's development and help the family contribute to this development. The intent of the law is to have the family and service providers work as a team to create, implement, and evaluate services that meet the needs of the disabled child while reflecting the concerns of the family and the available resources.

As is the case with the IEP, the IFSP is developed at a meeting that includes the child's parent or parents; other family members at the parent's request; an advocate or other non-family member (at the parent's request); the child's service coordinator; at least one person directly involved in conducting the evaluations and assessments; and, as appropriate, individuals who will be providing services to the child or family. The initial IFSP meetings and periodic reviews must be conducted in places and at times that are convenient for families and in the native language or other mode of communication used by the family. All arrangements for the meetings must be made far enough in advance to ensure that the team members will be able to attend, and written notice must be provided to the family and other team members.

In many other respects, the IFSP is similar to the IEP. It is a written document that describes:

- the child's present levels of physical development, cognitive development, communication development, social or emotional development, and adaptive development

- the family's resources, priorities, and concerns relating to enhancing the development of the child with a disability

- the major outcomes to be achieved for the child and the family; the criteria, procedures, and timelines used to determine progress; and whether modifications or revisions of the outcomes or services are necessary

- the specific early intervention services needed to meet the unique needs of the child and the family, including the frequency, intensity, and the method of delivering services

- the natural environments in which services will be provided, including an explanation why the services might not be provided in a natural environment

- the projected dates for initiation of services, which must be as soon as possible after the IFSP meeting, and the anticipated duration of the service

- any payment arrangements that are needed

- the name of the service coordinator assigned to the family (the coordinator is responsible for implementing the plan and coordinating with other agencies and persons)

- the steps involved in supporting the child's transition to preschool or other appropriate services, including parent training, future placement, adjustment strategies for the child, and communication with the LEA to ensure continuity of services

- medical and other needed services

The IFSP and IEP differ in a number of ways. The IFSP is family centered and includes family outcomes. It is oriented toward the natural environments, the home and community settings, so that everyday interventions can take place. The IFSP may also involve more agencies than an IEP and a family service coordinator.

Time Considerations

Once a public agency receives a referral, evaluations and assessments must be completed and a meeting held to develop an initial IFSP. As a rule, the IFSP is not developed until after the evaluation, nor are services provided. An exception is made for the child who has pressing needs and requires immediate services.

The IFSP must be reviewed every six months. Under some conditions or if requested by the family, the review may take place more often. The purpose of the review is to determine how much progress is being made toward the outcomes specified in the IFSP and if the outcomes or services should be modified. The IFSP team carries out the review in a meeting or through other agreed upon means. In addition, an annual review of the IFSP must be carried out during which recent assessment and other information are considered and any needed revisions to the IFSP undertaken.

Creating a Meaningful IFSP

The intent of the law is that the IFSP should be family-centered. For early intervention to be successful, it must match the needs of the child and fit the dynamics of the family. The professional members of the IFSP team should strive to build a positive relationship with the family and function as partners with them.

The natural environments of the disabled child and the family should form the basis of the IFSP. It is essential to identify these natural environments and note the routine ways in which the family and disabled child are engaged in the environments. The learning opportunities provided by the family, community, and nearby settings can contribute significantly to the development of the child and the positive relationship among the family members.

In addition, the focus on the natural environments increases the probability that the skills the child develops will be generalized to life situations and thus contribute to the future success of the child in and out of school. Even the most basic activities, for example a family trip to a park, can become a means of promoting language skills, coordination, social interaction, and familiarity with the community. Because the skills were practiced in a natural environment rather than in a classroom or therapy center, the child is more likely to use them in other situations and not associate the skills with the instructional or therapeutic setting. A related benefit is that skills developed and refined in the natural environment contribute to the independent functioning, a long-term goal for every child with a disability.

Suitable expected outcomes for the child should be developed as a result of an appropriate assessment and reflect the needs of the child, the resources available to the family, and the concerns and priorities of the family. These outcomes are best developed in collaboration with the family so that they are reasonable, valued by the family, and achievable. In addition the outcomes should contribute to the family's ability to enhance the child's experiences in everyday activities.

The members of the IFSP team should work together closely and identify the responsibilities each member will fulfill. On a regular basis, the members should evaluate how well they are accomplishing their responsibilities and be willing to adapt in order to ensure that the outcomes are being achieved. The IFSP team is not just a group of people who have been assigned tasks. Each member should be committed to

supporting the efforts of the team to enhance the family's ability to meet the developmental needs of the disabled child. This
willingness to work together is especially important to support
the key members of the team who spend the most time with
the disabled child.

VII

Evaluation and Placement Guidelines

The law has built several protections for the disabled student and for the parents regarding both testing and placement. To ensure fair treatment and responsible results, the following are required of the local education agency.

- A variety of assessment tools and strategies must be used, not a single measure.

- The assessments must gather relevant information about the disabled child's functional, developmental, and academic status.

- Assessments used must be technically sound and assess relevant cognitive, behavioral, physical, or developmental factors.

- Assessments must not be discriminatory on a racial or cultural basis.

- All evaluations must be conducted in the child's native language, unless it is not feasible to do so.

- Trained personnel should administer assessments and conduct other evaluation activities.

- The child should be assessed in all areas of suspected disability.

- When a child changes school districts, assessments must be coordinated in order to ensure timely and appropriate evaluations.

- Upon completion of the assessment process, including

observations, the determination of a disability and the identification of educational needs must be made by a team of qualified professionals and at least one parent.

In the most recent version of IDEA, an important change in the identification of children with specific learning disabilities has been included. Traditionally, a child was considered to have a learning disability if there was a severe discrepancy between achievement and intellectual ability in reading, listening, speaking, or mathematics. The use of such discrepancies is still permitted, but a second approach, response to intervention (RTI), is also allowed by the law.

Response to intervention (sometimes worded responsiveness to intervention) is a multi-stage technique based on how well students respond to instructional practices. Although there are several approaches to RTI, the general pattern is described below.

- Students are identified at possibly being at risk by a screening process, past performance, observations, or a combination of information sources.

- These students receive intense instruction as a supplement to the regular classroom activities. The supplemental instruction is conducted with evidence-based practices and materials. The students' progress is monitored on a regular basis.

- If students don't make adequate progress, additional instructional resources are brought into play, perhaps through a supplemental program outside the regular classroom. Progress monitoring is continued.

- Any students who fail to respond to the supplemental instruction are referred for evaluation. Supplemental instruction is maintained, along with progress monitoring.

- If the evaluation suggests that a child has a disability,

the child is referred for special education services. If the evaluation does not identify a disability, other forms of supplemental instruction are tried and the student's progress is monitored on a regular basis.

In developing the IEP, the team should consider the strengths of the child, the concerns of the parents, the most recent evaluation, and the academic, developmental, and functional needs of the child. In addition, a number of special factors must be considered:

- behavior that impedes the child's learning or that of other children
- limited English proficiency
- Braille or other media for a child who is blind or visually impaired
- communication needs for a child who is deaf or hearing impaired
- assistive technology devices and services

When considering the placement of the child for special education services, the IEP team must start with the least restrictive environment as the preferred option. In some circumstances, other placements in the continuum of services might be considered. A typical continuum of services is shown below. Note that this continuum will vary from location to location.

- regular classroom placement with supplemental services such as speech therapy
- regular classroom placement with support for the teacher from a special education staff member
- regular classroom placement with additional support through team teaching, co-teaching, or collaborative instruction

- regular classroom placement with part of the school day spent in a resource room

- individual support for the student with a disability by the special education teacher or other personnel through adaptations or modifications to the general education curriculum and assessments

- individualized or small group instruction either within the general education classroom or with pull-out resource services for specific skill development

- instruction in a self-contained environment in which specialized strategies and techniques are available with an alternative course of studies, including social, emotional, and behavioral skills

- vocational adjustment setting for students with a disability who are working part-time or who are receiving job training at a separate site

- home or hospital-based instruction for students who are confined because of a health condition that may or may not relate to the primary disability

- a separate program within a comprehensive school or separate facility, often in conjunction with other districts or service agencies, including correctional facilities

- for students whose needs exceed the resources traditionally available, approved nonpublic schools or special settings, including residential placement

The IEP team will also find it useful to discuss or specify the adaptations, modifications, or other changes to the placement of the child with a disability. It is often the case that some of the simplest changes can contribute greatly to the child's success in the classroom academically and socially. The following list is far from exhaustive, but provides some guidance about how the classroom experience for the disabled child can be improved.

- adapted worksheets and assignments
- arranging seating to facilitate the student's functioning
- audio presentation of text materials, when available
- audio recording of classroom instruction or discussions
- buddy system to promote social interaction skills during non-academic school activities
- extra time to dress for PE
- learning partner assistance with comprehension of curricular materials
- lowered difficulty level of instructional or practice material
- modifying content of assignments
- paraprofessional or peer escorts to classes at beginning of semester
- periodic comprehension checks of reading material
- periodic review of playground rules by teacher or yard supervisor
- pre-teaching/re-teaching
- provisions for time to take medication
- rearranging the classroom to avoid mobility problems
- shorter assignments
- use of graphic organizers
- use of supplementary materials

VIII

Preparing the IEP—A Group Process

In a sense, an IEP is something like using a road map to take a trip. It has a starting place, a defined route, and a destination.

The Starting Point

The law is very clear that the information which shapes the IEP must come from a variety of sources. The sources, generally, are:

1. **Observations**, for example,

    *   by previous teachers of the child

    *   by other professionals who have seen the child, such as
            the pediatrician
            the school nurse

    *   by the yard duty supervisor

    *   by the school secretary

    *   by the child's teacher, as the child attempts to
            follow directions
            listen
            attend
            generalize learnings
            speak

    *   by an evaluation of work samples

    *   by the parents

2. **Records**, for example,

    *   developmental history of milestones, such as

age of crawling
age of walking
age of spoken language
age of preferred handedness

- case histories on the child, prepared by others

- medical records from specialists who have examined the child

- school records

- health records

- social/emotional relationships
  in the family
  in the neighborhood
  at school

3. **Testing**, for example,

- achievement, criterion and norm-referenced, aptitude, spelling, reading, mathematics, handwriting

- vision

- hearing

- perceptual

- associative

- language

- vocational

- motor/neurological

4. **From the child**, for example,

- interests

- hobbies

- use of free time

- favorite television programs

- best friends

- aspirations

- self-concept

Obviously, within each category, many other items could be listed. This is only a framework for considering the multiple possibilities for initial input. What should emerge is a pattern of the child's learning strengths and weaknesses. How does the child learn? What modality does the child appear to prefer, or does a preferred modality exist?

Since the law is clear in stating that scores alone are not enough in making judgments about a child's learning styles, the following factors must be considered:

1. Do you know the tests sufficiently well to know what they are measuring and how they are doing it?

    For example, there are many, many "reading" tests, but what is the child called upon to do in those used?

- Orally read a word in isolation?

- Orally read a paragraph?

- Silently read a paragraph and answer questions about it?

- Silently define words?

- Silently read a passage with words missing?

2. Do you have comparisons of the child's performance on different ways of testing the same skill?

    For example, in reading, could you sample performance in two or more reading tests as listed above?

- Were the tests timed?
  If so, were you able to compare timed against untimed performance to get a "speed" versus "power" differential?

3. Can you determine through which channels the child appears to learn best? Were there significant differences in tests in which the child:

   - heard and then wrote, or drew, or moved (auditory-motor) or, saw and then orally responded (visual-vocal) or, saw and then moved, or wrote, or drew (visual-motor) or,

   - did the child function best when all learning modalities were available, that is, auditory, visual, vocal, and tactile-kinesthetic?

4. What would happen (or did happen) when you required a verbal instead of a motor response to a test item?

Since tests should be administered only in the manner in which they were standardized, variations in administration should be done only after the standard administration. If this is not possible because of the condition of the child, clearly state this when the results are recorded and report any changes in the administration procedure.

An understanding, in plotting a profile of the student's strengths and weaknesses, of milestones in growth and development (cognitive, linguistic, perceptual, motoric, for example) becomes an important tool in organizing a learning program. Did the child meet the milestones at approximately the anticipated time? How have these affected learning characteristics in terms of the suspected or recognized disability of the child? In addition, an understanding of sequences in academic learning is critical if a meaningful program for the child is to be developed.

IX

Beginning the IEP

Teachers have found that the use of a simple, informal worksheet (or series of them assigned to specific curricular areas, for example, reading, math, etc.) can be invaluable in beginning to state, in written form, the program for the student.

The model worksheet below allows for notes, scribbling, erasures, additions, cross-outs, and anything else that is needed to prepare a working draft of the program.

Worksheet for IEP Preparation			
Student:_____Curricular Area:_____			
STRENGTHS Can Do Likes To Do Interests	CHALLENGES Difficult Areas	WHY	BASED ON

1. **Strengths.** This includes everything that can be mentioned that will affect programing for the student, such as:

   • interested in rocket ships

   • enjoys coloring

   • watches situation comedies on TV

   • likes to go to the market with a parent

   • collects stamps

- sings simple tunes
- knows the alphabet
- recognizes fifteen words at sight, etc.

2. **Challenges.** Suggested notations might include:

- tires after five minutes
- is confused with a series of three directions
- needs to trace alphabet letters before naming them
- has difficulty with the "s" and "f" sounds in conversational speech
- can ride a two-wheel bicycle only with difficulty

3. **Why.** This may be the most difficult question to answer because at the time of this worksheet preparation, full information from parents and the evaluation team may not yet be available. Possibilities, however, such as the following could be offered:

- poor eye-hand coordination
- weak muscle tone
- no clear lateral preferences, etc.

4. **Based On.** Here, back-up information should be stated, such as:

- observations
- statements made by the student
- information from parents
- information in the cumulative files
- observations made by previous teachers, etc.

X
Goals and Objectives

Once there is an understanding of how the child learns and of the specific needs and strengths of the child, then it is possible to lay out goals and objectives. You know what you are dealing with, and you can now determine how you will use this information.

A goal is a point to which effort is directed. It is a statement of general intent. Embedded in that definition is a way of knowing that the destination has been reached.

General goals:
Jason wants to learn to type.
Susan wants to learn to play the piano.
Pat wants to travel.

Specific goals :
Jason wants to type 70 words a minute.
Susan wants to play Chopin's *Scherzo No. 4 in E.*
Pat wants to see Paris.

Objectives, both short and long term, sequential and concurrent, provide a systematic sequence of the skills needed to achieve the goal. For the purposes of the IEP, objectives must be as specific as possible and state:

- to what degree of success the skill will be performed,

- by what date this will be achieved, and

- a learning channel, directly or indirectly

Weak objective:
Juana will learn the alphabet.

61

Outside of the fact that a date and level of competency are missing, the objective fails to indicate whether Johnny must sing it, say it, recognize the letters (cursive or manuscript?) in sequence, tactually organize it, etc.

Better objective:
>Juana will be able to say the alphabet in sequence without assistance in eight out of ten trials, by November 15.

Many educators agree that seventy percent success as a criterion is acceptable, though, in some cases, the IEP team may feel that absolute accuracy (one hundred percent) is necessary if the next objective (or stage) is to be commenced. There are few circumstances in which absolute accuracy is necessary for a student to progress to the next skill in a sequence.

In laying out objectives, factors such as the child's learning characteristics, age, disabling condition, and current skill levels will determine whether they are to be sequential, concurrent, or a mixture of both. In addition, the subject area may also have bearing on the decision.

For a program of mathematical concepts, there is a distinct hierarchy that will dictate the sequential nature of the objectives. A child should learn basic addition facts before learning to add two-digit numbers with regrouping. In contrast, for handwriting instruction, the sequence of skills is not so well defined. Certainly, some strokes are easier than others, but it would be difficult to specify that the cursive letter *b* should be mastered before the cursive letter *h* is attempted.

Examples of goals:

- By June 15, Bill will be able to read at grade level 4.5 as measured by the Phonics-Based Reading Test.

- By June 15, Sarah will be able to spell at grade

level 6.6 as measured by the Wide Range Achievement Test, Level 11.

- By June 15, Edie will achieve at a fourth grade level in arithmetic as measured by the Test of Mathematical Abilities.

Examples of objectives:

- By November 1, Johnny will, on lined paper, be able to write, in cursive, the following letters, with consistent slant, and spacing, *t, f, k, c, o, e, m, n, g, b, d.*

- By January 15, Bill will be able to read the following words, in isolation, immediately upon presentation: come, look, with, open, him, their, play.

- By November 15, Sarah will be able to correctly solve 7 out of 10 subtraction problems, all with sums less than 10, in three minutes.

- By March 1, Barbara will be able to spell, in written form, 15 out of 20 words, selected at random, from the first half of the Dolch Word List.

Goals are generally planned on the basis of a full year of educational programing, unless there is a multi-year IEP. As a result, there will be fewer stated goals in an IEP than there will be stated short and long term objectives. There is no ratio of objectives to goals. In some cases only one objective may be linked to one goal. In other cases, there may be an entire sequence of objectives that are seen as sequential steps in the realization of a single goal.

Areas generally designated as goals, but always dependent on the student's specific learning profile, may include:
- reading
- spelling

- handwriting
- language arts
- mathematics
- career education
- pre-vocational and vocational education
- physical education
- motor development
- the arts
- social/emotional development
- language development and speech
- recreation
- occupational/physical therapy
- independent living skills

Also of concern are factors such as the possible need for counseling and other related services either for the student or for the parents.

XI

IEP Checklist

Regardless of the form the written IEP takes—and there are hundreds of different ones in use across the country—the law makes clear what should be included.

The required elements of the IEP are:

1. the present levels of academic achievement and functional performance

2. a statement of measurable annual goals, both academic and functional

3. a description of how the child's progress toward meeting the annual goals will be measured and when periodic progress reports will be made

4. specific educational services to be provided, based on peer-reviewed research to the extent practicable

5. an explanation, if any, of why the child will not participate with nondisabled children in the regular class and other activities

6. a statement of any accommodations that are necessary to measure the academic achievement and functional performance of the child on state and district assessments

7. projected date for initiation of the services and their frequency, location, and duration

8. for the first IEP after the child turns 16, a statement of measurable postsecondary goals and transition services

The most basic information to be included in the IEP is the initial evaluation that determined the child's disability or the most recent evaluation. This information should include:

- what tests were administered

- when the tests were administered

- who administered the tests

The evaluation information should reflect both academic achievement and functional performance. If the student has participated in state or district assessments, these results should be indicated, also.

In order to meet goals through specific educational approaches, related services, such as counseling, sensory-integration, one-to-one remediation, or visual and auditory training may be necessary. These must be spelled out.

A time line may be a convenient way to visually represent when specific services should be initiated and concluded. This can be a distinct aid to written preparation of the IEP. It can also show sequences of learning or overlapping of services. A sample initial information form can be found on page 70.

The format on the next page is one way to organize the educational content of the IEP. Again, this is one suggestion. states and school districts will undoubtedly have forms they recommend.

Subject Area

Present level of performance *(years/months when possible):*

_____

Based on the following tests: *(spell out the names—do not use abbreviations)*:

    administered on:_____

    administered by:_____

Goal *(years/months when possible):*

    to be reached by (date):_____

As indicated by (tests listed):

_____

_____

_____

_____

_____

_____

_____

Sample Reading Form

Present level of performance:

- Grade level 4.5, Wide Range Achievement Test, Level I, word recognition section, administered 9/15/05 by Dr. Sorenson;

- Grade level 3.1, Nelson Reading Test, Form A, administered 9/12/05 by Bea Whitemore;

- Grade level 3.6, Gray Oral Reading Test, Form A, administered 9/12/05, by Bea Whitemore.

- Can read slowly with the assistance of a partner the selections in Open Court Reading.

Goal:

By June, 2005, will achieve at: 5.5 in oral decoding, as measured by a retest on the Wide Range Achievement Test, Level 1; 4.0, on Form B of the Nelson Reading Test; 4.4 on the Gray Oral Reading Test, Form B; and complete, without assistance, the final selection in the Open Court Reading series.

At this point, based on a variety of information sources, not solely test scores, and including observations and class-room assessments, the team must determine what the child will need to meet the goal.

- What sequence of education objectives must be developed?

- Who will be responsible for each of the objectives?

- When will each related learning activity be intiated?

- When should each be terminated?

- What related services will be required?

- What special provisions, in light of the student's special learning characteristics, should be made?

- What methods or approaches should be employed to teach the student?

Example 1

Objective:	Steven will be able to say the alphabet, in correct sequence, with no assistance, by October 15.
Who:	Mrs. Martha Smith will work daily with him for ten minutes.
Starting Date:	September 25.
Materials/Method:	Sing the Alphabet Song with the CD.
	Sing the Alphabet Song without the CD.
	Use the tape recorder, first to listen with; then to speak along with.
	Use the tape recorder to tape the alphabet by himself with assistance.
Evaluation:	To say the alphabet correctly in sequence.

Example 2

Objective:	Victoria will be able to print her first and last names correctly on lined paper, by November 1.
Who:	Mr. Roberto Gonzales to supervise a volunteer on daily basis for ten minutes, starting October 1.

Materials/Method:	Finger painting to "feel" the strokes of the letters, (classroom).
	Chalkboard activities with top-to-bottom and left-to-right training in strokes (classroom).
	Motor training with Bob Jones, in remedial PE, to enhance gross motor development, and shoulder girdle freedom (three times a week for twenty minutes each period).
	Visual therapy with Dr. Weber to enhance eye tracking (scheduling to be arranged with Dr. Weber).
	Art with Mrs. Ryan (the art teacher) daily, for thirty minutes, in a small group, for clay work to enhance finger dexterity.
	Mr. Reilly, the volunteer, to guide her hand, in writing each letter daily, for ten minutes.
Evaluation:	Print her full name on lined paper.

Example 3

Objective:	Sharonna will solve eight out of ten arithmetic problems correctly, on a silent five-minute test dealing with multiplication of two-digit numbers, by January 15.
Who:	Mr. Green, her special class teacher, starting November 4, or immediately after she can recite, in order, the two times tables to 2 x 12.

Method:	Cuisenaire Rods used daily for twenty minutes with Mr. Green. Manipulative activities involving grouping by twos. Card and board games which involve two jumps, responding by twos. Jumprope activities that require two jumps to a count at recess.
	Doubling simple recipes at home with her mother.
	Verbalizing as she works individual problems in the special classroom.
	Work every other day, with an older student-tutor for ten minutes.
	Complete worksheets from *Real Math*, untimed, weekly.
Evaluation:	Five-minute/timed math test, by January 15, in which she will correctly solve eight out of ten problems as stated in the objective.

Obviously, one of the most difficult and demanding challenges related to preparing an IEP is that of developing sequential objectives. To do so requires not only a knowledge of child growth and development, but also a knowledge of the sequential nature of academic programing and the unique learning characteristics and needs of the child. It means that the teacher must know how, for example, reading or mathematical skills develop in the child, and by what process the child learns. It means that reading or mathematics must be broken down into skill sequences. Moreover, it requires that the critical team members understand what the child can do, what the child has difficulty with, and why.

Sample: Initial Information on the Form

Child's full name_____Male/Female____

Nickname_____ Date of birth____Age (yrs/mos)____

Grade____or entering grade____School_____

School year_____School district_____

This form prepared by_____

Evaluation/Screening committee

_____

_____

_____

Date of meeting_____

Attending:

Name_____Position_____

Name_____Position_____

Name_____Position_____

Name_____Position_____

Status of visual skills *(last examination, by whom, results):*

_____

_____

_____

Status of auditory skills *(last examination, by whom, results):*

_____

_____

_____

continued

72

Status of neurological and/or motor skills *(last examination, by whom, results):*

_____

_____

_____

Brief review of educational history:

_____

_____

_____

Health status:

_____

_____

_____

Other pertinent information *(vocational, social, emotional, psychological, familial, developmental, etc.):*

_____

_____

_____

The program has been read and approved by the committee:

_____

_____

_____

The program is _____ is not _____ acceptable to the parents.

The program is _____ is not _____ acceptable to the student.

Parent_____Date_____

Parent_____Date_____

Student's signature *(when appropriate):*

_____Date_____

XII
Relating Tests and Observations
to Goal and Objective Writing

In order to prepare sequentially organized objectives, there is no substitute for knowing the wide range of factors that are associated with each of the tool subjects—that is, reading, handwriting, language arts, and mathematics.

For some of these factors there are tests that measure the child's efficiency. For others, there are no adequate tests. Here, only observations will indicate the child's specific needs. For example, there are tests that describe a child's ability to decode words as compared with other students. But, there are no tests that measure how willing a child is to complete a written assignment.

The initial and subsequent evaluations of a child are usually carried out by a multidisciplinary team. The child's evaluation should include assessments of all areas of suspected disability, including, where appropriate, health, vision, hearing, social and emotional status, general intelligence, academic performance, communicative status, and motor abilities. The assessments shall not be racially or culturally discriminating and shall be administered in the child's native language.

As an aid to the teacher and diagnostician, the following pages contain an analysis of four critical subject areas. The analysis reflects requirements, that is, what is needed in the learner for efficiency at that task; observations, general and specific, that can be made by the teacher as the child is engaged in the task; and general areas of testing that will reveal in-depth learning needs related to that subject.

The items included in this informal overview are not intended to represent a full listing. Those included are not listed in terms of degree of importance. In addition, factors such as self-concept, general health, the impact of nutrition on learning efficiency, family values regarding learning, and so on, must be considered as part of a meaningful evaluation.

Handwriting

Requirements:

- visual pursuit ability
- eye/hand coordination
- finger strength
- finger dexterity
- spatial awareness
- spatial organization
- visual convergence
- visual recall
- proprioceptive recall
- body image
- body awareness
- recognition of basic geometric shapes
- reproduction of basic shapes
- visualization
- form perception
- auditory/motor integration
- spatial integration (top/bottom; left/right; front/back, etc.)

- wrist rotation ability
- organized lateral preferences
- bilateral controls
- postural organization (vestibular, muscular)
- tactile efficiency
- motor planning and generalizations

General observations (while the child writes):
- curve of the back
- tilt of the head
- distance of the head from the paper
- tilt of the pencil
- grasp on the pencil
- positioning of the helping hand
- placement of the feet and legs
- kinesthetic overflow (tongue or other movements)
- rhythm of writing
- level of the shoulders
- total degree of body muscle tone

Specific observations (while the child writes):
- preferred form (manuscript or cursive)
- formation of letters
- spacing of letters
- spacing of words

- reversals of letters
- reversals of words
- relationship of sizes
- total slant of finished copy
- positioning of the paper
- relationship of ascenders to descenders
- presence of margins

Tests (generically indicated):

- awareness of right and left: on self; on others; with letters and words
- visual-perceptual skills
- muscle tone tests
- ability to reproduce two-dimensional geometric representations
- ability to copy on both lined and unlined paper, both far to near point, and near to near point
- postural integration tests
- visual efficiency testing
- ocular pursuit testing
- letter recognition testing

Spelling

Requirements:

- auditory discrimination
- auditory memory

- auditory sequencing
- visual memory
- visual discrimination
- visual sequencing
- auditory receptive vocabulary
- spatial awareness and understanding
- speech efficiency
- temporal awareness
- visualization
- ability to make cross-modality matches (e.g., auditory-visual, visual-motor, etc.)
- phonic skills
- ability to generalize, e.g., shapes, motoric, etc.
- tactile/kinesthetic abilities
- motor planning skills

Observations:
- forgets words almost immediately
- poor reading ability
- poor ability to blend words while pronouncing them
- must spell orally as words are written
- misspells without consistency
- misspells with consistency
- omits/adds/substitutes letters
- does/doesn't recognize a misspelled word

- learns words only if they are traced several times
- difficulty in following spatial directions
- underdeveloped sense of laterality (left/right awareness)
- difficulty in sounding out new words
- reversals apparent in spelling
- restricted speaking vocabulary
- mispronounces words in conversational speech
- spells better orally than in writing
- has to repeat things to remember them

Tests (generically indicated):
- standardized spelling achievement test
- dictation test
- testing of phonetic versus non-phonetic words
- auditory receptive vocabulary
- test of sequential auditory memory, with digits and words
- phonics skills
- laterality tests (left/right awareness on self, others, letters, and words)
- memory test for sentence recall
- auditory blending and auditory analysis skills
- auditory discrimination
- auditory acuity (pure tone testing)
- standardized reading test, both comprehension and

word meanings

- visualization skills
- measurement of ability to recognize correctly from incorrectly spelled words
- an oral test of spelling
- rhyming concepts
- motor sequencing testing
- visual recall
- spatial awareness and understanding

Reading

Requirements:

- visual acuity
- binocular convergence and focusing skills when material is at close range
- visual tracking ability
- directional organization
- auditory receptive vocabulary
- perceptual organization in all senses
  figure-ground
  closure
  discrimination
  memory
  form
- phonetic understandings and generalizations
- sound/symbol relationships
- sequentiality concepts

- imagery
- visualization
- postural integration
- spatial awareness and understandings (top/bottom, front/back, etc.)
- body awareness and body image
- auditory and visual rhyming
- lateral stability (preferred side, left/right awareness)

Observations:

- difficulty in consistently associating a sound with a symbol
- repeating words in oral reading/skipping words in oral reading
- skipping lines in oral reading
- decoding skills high/comprehension low
- decoding skills low/comprehension high
- mispronounces words
- remembers ideas/forgets facts
- forgets ideas/remembers facts
- word calling (cannot recall either ideas or facts)
- must read orally to recall information
- forgets words from day to day
- leans too close to the book
- awkward position while reading

- tires easily, quickly when reading
- points when reading
- noticeably subvocalizes when reading

Tests (generically indicated):

- test of oral reading
- decoding test
- sound/symbol testing
- rapid naming of pictures
- visualization
- understands word opposites
- visual perception skills
- auditory perception skills
- visual acuity and binocular skills
- auditory acuity
- speech testing
- listening ability
- laterality testing (left/right on self; on others; with letters; with words)
- sequencing skill
- motor skills testing

Mathematics

Requirements:

- understanding of time awareness and understanding of space (top/bottom; left/right; etc.)

- visualization
- one-to-one correspondence
- ability to estimate space
- body awareness
- body image
- body rhythm
- ability to reason
- visual and auditory recall
- sequentiality concepts
- lateral organization
- motor planning ability
- ability to generalize
- ability to count sequentially
- ability to group objects

Observations:
- difficulty in recalling numerical sequences
- miscounts concrete objects
- crowds problems on a math sheet
- difficulty in recalling basic math facts
- "learns" a process but forgets it quickly
- confused by borrowing and carrying
- difficulty in reading numerals, i.e., writes them backwards
- difficulty in properly writing numerals

- confused on: before/after; big/little; now/then, etc.
- requires "aids" such as finger counting, tapping, etc., while doing math work
- confused in motor acts,
- appears awkward
- works slowly
- verbalizes while doing math
- distinct motor overflow difficulties

Tests (generically indicated):

- standardized test of mathematical competency (should include money, measurement, word problems, etc.)
- test of reasoning ability
- laterality testing
- motor testing (posture, spatial, planning, etc.)
- visualization testing
- numeral recognition testing
- numeral naming testing
- visual and auditory recall testing
- time telling testing
- testing of sequentiality concepts

XIII

Implementing the IEP

Once the evaluation has been completed and an analysis of the child's learning characteristics undertaken, goals and objectives can be specified. The next step is identifying the instructional practices and support needed to achieve the goals. These practices and support must be stated in the IEP. To reiterate what has already been said, goals are established not solely on the basis of tests. The determination of goals must come from a variety of sources.

Remedial specialists, diagnosticians, and others working directly with disabled children and adults recognize that there are three general approaches that may be used in special programs:

- direct work on the skill or area of need

- preliminary work on the antecedents for that skill

- a combination of the above

An array of methods, materials, and programs are available to educators to develop or enhance specific skill areas. There is not space in this handbook to discuss at any length the process of material selection. Suffice it to say that the selection of material should be based on certain criteria, such as:

- Is it based on practices that are research-based?

- Will it do what it purports to do?

- Does it have flexibility, that is, can it be used in other ways?

- Does the price warrant its purchase?

- Does it have a long life or is it consumable?

Some goals and objectives will not require anything other than the teacher's resourcefulness and creativity. For example, consider the goal for Jimmy of developing by June three independent living functions: dressing himself, making purchases that total less than $1.00, and using the telephone to make outgoing calls. Let's say that under dressing himself, one specific objective is that Jimmy will be able to tie his shoelaces independently.

The Methods/Materials section of the IEP is, then, the *how* part of the program. It describes the ways that will be used to accomplish the objective, which in turn will meet the needs of the general goal.

In the Methods/Materials section of the IEP, there may be several items listed for this one objective:

Objective	Methods/Materials
Jimmy will be able to tie his own shoelaces by June.	1. Daily work with Mrs. Jones, using a large piece of yarn over his own thigh
	2. Finger manipulation activities to increase dexterity and independent finger tone, using clay and play ground equipment
	3. Eye tracking activities to enhance coordination, using wall targets, daily, in a small group, for three minute periods
	4. Eye-hand coordination through

88

activities such as pegboard work; threading cardboard, during art periods

5. Using the large shoe in the room to tie, at least every other day

6. Having parents monitor at home some weekly practice sessions so that Jimmy can demonstrate his progress

Here, because of the nature of the close relationship between the specific objective and the goal, the requisites of stated degree of success and learning channel are embedded in the task itself. What is important to note is that Jimmy was receiving assistance by a combination of direct training and training in the skills that undergird the process of tying shoelaces. If Jimmy were to achieve completion of the skill, that is, independent ability to tie his own shoelaces, even if loosely, prior to June, then all the better. If, however, it appears that this skill is so demanding that a June completion is unrealistic, then at a meeting of the IEP team, an adjustment in the IEP might be made. The adjustment might be one in which the statement is modified to: Jimmy will learn to thread his shoelaces independently. That is, only one segment is determined to be the objective for that time period. Then, when the annual required evaluation of the IEP program is made, a new determination can be stated for the following school year.

Needless to say, because the need for modifications will indeed occur, IEPs should always be easily accessible to those working directly with the child. A truly responsive program requires that all those involved with the student have their own copy immediately available for use. Storage at some point other than easy and immediate access to staff defeats the purpose of ongoing use of the program. Storage should always protect the child and family and adhere to the principles of confidentiality.

In other areas, including the academic, hands-on manipulative multisensory activities, under the Methods/Materials section, can remedially help the students attain the desired outcome. For example, let's say that the goal is: Susan will recognize ten words, immediately upon presentation, in random order, each presented on a single card in manuscript, by June. An objective might be, because of Susan's learning characteristics and needs: Susan will correctly name each letter of the lower-case alphabet upon presentation, one-hundred percent of the time. One approach would be to train Susan for the task by daily review of small clusters of lower-case letters until she achieves the stated criterion of one-hundred percent. If it works, this is fine. If, on the other hand, Susan appears confused and forgets, and there is no appreciable improvement in her letter recognition, then attacking the objective by looking at the underlying skills will be in order.

Under the *how* section of the IEP, activities such as the following should be stated: tracing very large letters at the chalkboard, tracing sandpaper letters at her desk, development of lateral preferences, making letters out of clay, use of fingerpainting (the letters), feeling and saying the letters, walking-out the letters (on the schoolyard), etc. Tapping into other sensory channels helps the disabled child integrate his or her learnings.

One final note on the matter of Methods/Materials is that of incorporating within the child's program a way or ways to determine whether the child can transfer the skill to a different setting. A problem that plagues remedial specialists is the child who will appear to have "learned" a specific task in the remedial setting, but who returns home or to a home classroom, and is not able to do what has just been "learned." Or the child who has "learned" ten sight words, on flash cards, but who sees them on different colored paper stock and doesn't recognize them, or who "learns" them on the chalkboard but doesn't recognize them on the flash cards, etc. Such training has been identified as "splintering." That is, a specific task is "learned" and can be used only under specific conditions. Allowance, therefore, should be planned for altering the learning environment, from time to time, to determine whether that skill is truly a part of the learner. It is to avoid this problem that so much emphasis in the new IDEA has been placed on naturalistic environments and least restrictive environments. The more natural the learning environment, the more likely the child will be to generalize skills to varied situations.

XIV

Sequences in Learning

Any listing of learning "sequences" is difficult to prepare because skills do not develop in a precise order. Often, many skills are simultaneously developing in the child. Social, intellectual, emotional, sensory, health, biochemical, attentional, neurological, and perceptual factors all affect the learning process.

The following lists are more remedial than they are developmental because they move from small to larger, more complex and involved components. Remedial education, by its nature and definition, requires an analysis of needs followed by breaking down skills into small, finite units, each of which is taught or "developed." The range of skill units is then integrated into one whole process. For example, many children may come to school in either kindergarten or first grade recognizing words such as "milk" because it is such a common food. Remedially, for an older youngster, such a word is learned as a series of sound-units and then blended as a sight-recognition vocabulary was developed. In brief, the analysis is one of part-to-whole and whole-to-part relationships.

The lists are provided so that the teacher may sort out from the information about the child's learning characteristics what the child is able to do so that objectives may be properly organized.

What is important to remember is that the "tool" subjects—reading, spelling, handwriting, and mathematics—are means to an end. They help us survive—socially and economically.

They help us solve problems, locate necessary information, or do better at another task. It is far too easy to become so intensely focused on developing, for example, reading skills, that little opportunity is offered the child to use the skills to find out more about computers or how the planets revolve around the sun or how to repair an engine. Applying skills is just as important as learning or practicing them, so the IEP should include opportunities to apply what they have learned.

The "test" that a skill is being developed, or that an objective is being met outside of the evaluation required in the new law, is that the child can generalize or use that skill in a new setting. Usually the best way to determine this is to know the child so well that the child's interests can be positively applied to academic learning needs.

A second factor to keep in mind, again depending on the child, the learning background, and learning needs, is that only one objective might be enough for that child to master in a full year, rather than a series of them. Where there are intense learning disabilities, it is far better to take on fewer objectives, and to allocate the time for multiple opportunities to both build the skill and to use it in a variety of ways.

A third factor of importance in teaching the disabled child is that objectives can do double or triple duty. For example, while learning to recognize letter shapes, the child may also be developing handwriting skills. While learning to recognize his or her name, the child is learning to spell. One of the challenges of creating a meaningful IEP is the way in which the curriculum can be organized so that there is a unification of objectives through careful programming.

Reading

Learning-to-Read Skills:

- sings the alphabet
- says the alphabet
- discriminates straight from curved lines
- discriminates diagonal lines
- differentiates letters
- recognizes own name
- can name letters
- can give sounds to letters that are seen
- can give sounds to letters that are heard
- can give letter name to a letter sound that is heard
- can hear a letter sound and point to the letter in print
- can recognize initial consonant sounds in spoken words
- can recognize final consonant sounds in spoken words
- is developing a sight recognition vocabulary
- is able to discriminate short and long vowel sounds
- is able to rhyme one-syllable words
- is able to blend sounds into whole words
- is able to delete a specific sound from words that are heard and say the new word
- can pronounce blends in isolation
- can recognize blends in words that are heard
- can recognize blends in words that are seen

- hears syllables within multisyllabic words
- knows that variant spellings may make the same sound
- able to sound out new words
- has an understanding of phonetic generalizations

Reading-to-Learn Skills:
- gets the main idea of what has been read
- recalls facts into a proper sequence
- differentiates facts from opinions
- understands the relationship of supporting details to the main idea
- can draw inferences from what has been read
- defines new words from context
- is able to scan for specific information

Because most students who are having difficulty in reading are in the learning-to-read stage, it is here that associated skills must be explored. The status of developmental skills such as left-right differentiation, visual memory for letters and words, auditory memory for sounds and words, visualization and imagery skills, auditory (receptive) vocabulary, speech, size (spatial) relationships, eye-teaming and eye-tracking skills, and motor skills, should be determined and used as methods to develop the stated objectives in the child's IEP.

Spelling
- understands the concept of one thing following another
- can recall simple rhymes and verses
- pronounces words correctly, age and disability considered

- can visually recognize the difference between similar appearing letters
- can visually recognize the difference between similar appearing words
- can recognize left and right on the child
- can recognize left and right on objects
- can correctly name letters
- can write his or her name
- remembers address and telephone number
- remembers words the child has learned to read
- can write words when spelled orally
- can hear a sequence of letters and then write a word from memory
- has developed a spelling vocabulary of words
- writes sentences without assistance
- writes short stories
- remembers spelling words after the regular test
- uses spelling to make interests and needs known

Handwriting

- has established a preferred hand
- holds pencil properly
- has efficient sitting position
- understands top and bottom of the paper
- understands spatial concepts, such as big/little, tall/short, fat/thin, etc.

- is able to hold a visual fixation
- can have eyes tell hands what to do
- can properly make strokes top to bottom, left to right
- "helping hand" properly holds writing medium flat
- connects strokes in letters that require more than one stroke
- can copy the basic geometric shapes
- copies letters on the same paper
- copies from letters on the chalkboard
- understands left/right concepts
- recognizes properly executed from improperly executed letters
- produces manuscript letters with similar forms properly
- spaces letters properly
- spaces words properly
- writes consistently in manuscript or cursive

Mathematics

- knows concept of "one" and "more than one"
- can orally, sequentially count to a specific number
- understands spatial concepts such as big/little, more/less, before/after, etc.
- can properly copy numerals
- can name numerals through a specified number
- understands the concept of equivalencies

- has the concept of one-to-one correspondences
- has established body rhythm
- tells time to the hour
- tells time to the minute
- is able to group concrete objects
- translates a math problem into a drawing
- understands that sequential counting is "plus one"
- can count backwards, sequentially, from a specified number
- understands that counting backward is "take away one"
- can count by twos
- understands the concepts of weights and measurements
- can recognize, without counting, groups of a specified number
- can add to sums of five or less, in writing
- can add to sums of five or less, orally
- understands additive and subtractive relationships of numbers
- can subtract from numbers up to five, in writing
- can subtract from numbers up to five, orally
- can add to sums of ten or less, in writing
- can add to sums of ten or less, orally
- can subtract from numbers up to ten, in writing
- can subtract from numbers up to ten, orally
- can add to sums of twenty or less, in writing

- can add to sums of twenty or less, orally
- can subtract from numbers up to twenty, in writing
- can subtract from numbers up to twenty, orally
- groups and multiples by twos (and so on)
- separates and divides by twos (and so on)
- understands whole/part relationships
- can change money
- uses fractions—same denominator—different denominator
- understands decimals
- averages numbers

Where there are other areas that have been identified as being of importance to the student, specific objectives can be organized in terms of behavioral goals. For example, vocational planning objectives can be developed that are coordinated with the program: use of specific tools, following directions, being on time, filling out application forms, how to get to and from the place of work, getting along with others, etc., all become part of that program. Other behaviors—be they perceptual, motor, or social—also can be described in specific terms, as the learner's needs warrant.

XV

IEP Considerations

In meeting to review the specific needs of the child and in preparing the IEP, the team will want to consider other dimensions of the teaching-learning process for that child. These factors include any approaches, methods, services, or ways that will assist in fulfilling goals determined for that child. Some factors that should be considered are the following:

1. **Cross-Age Tutoring.** Are there students in the school who are capable of both providing social assistance at and after school and assisting with specific academic needs? Quite often, cross-age tutoring not only benefits the recipient, but the student-tutor as well. When utilized, student tutors should be carefully screened, trained, and observed so that the relationship is positive and helpful.

2. **Provisions for Recess and Lunch.** Can the student adequately manage independently getting to and from the classroom, and to the lavatory and drinking fountain at recesses and lunch periods? Are there hazards such as small hallways, physical barriers, excessive student crowding at specific points along the route? Will there be proper management of the time so that while the student is with others, he or she is participating with them?

3. **Learning Stations.** In both the regular and special classroom, are these well organized so that the student can benefit from the activities designed for the stations? Is the student one who can work independently, or does the activity require monitoring? Is the material regularly changed and updated to maintain student interest and progress?

4. **Learning Structure.** Are there, or will there be, planned and ample opportunities, on a regular basis, for independent learning, small group activities, and large group participation? Is the room sufficiently organized, with materials in reach or property stored, so that the student feels organized? Are work samples properly maintained?

5. **Multisensory Learnings.** Is there a sufficient variety of material to stimulate learning by approaching other-than-traditional learning channels? For example, are there ways provided to reach the student with visual-auditory-tactile input simultaneously? Are there provisions for approaching learning through the auditory channels, and then later blending with the visual through the use of tape recordings? Are there adequate amounts of clay or fingerpaints?

6. **Volunteers.** Is there a school list of volunteers or is the parent-teacher association able to provide volunteers on a regular basis? Have they been given an orientation to the needs of the child and what the disabling condition is all about? Is there a library of material that is available on loan for volunteers? Is there a consistent, ongoing training program? Have local volunteer agencies or service organizations been tapped for assistance?

7. **Community Specialists.** Should the student require services that cannot be adequately or properly provided by the local public agency, is there a listing of specialists who could provide needed services? For example, who in the community could provide specific remedial education on a one-to-one basis, or visual therapy, or counseling, or other related services?

8. **Curriculum Services.** Within the local education agency, what resources are available, in the way of specialized textbooks, training aids, and materials for use by and with the student? If such items are not in the curriculum depart-

ment, there may be ways of obtaining them on a loan or rental basis, from an adjoining school district.

9. **Retired Teachers**. Teachers who have retired may often be quite eager to have some contact with children. If your state teachers' organization has a local office, you may be able to make contact with those who have specific training in a needed curriculum area, or you may be able to contact someone through your local school district offices. It's a resource that shouldn't be overlooked.

10. **Service Organizations**. Quite often local groups such as the Elks, Kiwanis, Lions, Clipped Wings, Easter Seals Society, or United Cerebral Palsy, are delighted to make not only services but specific pieces of equipment available for use in classes for the disabled. Should there be expensive pieces of equipment that would be useful in certain settings, prepare a list of what is needed, what use it will be put to, its cost, and how it may be obtained, and call on the agencies, inviting representatives to see what is going on in their community.

11. **Community Resources**. It has been made very clear by the U.S. Department of Education that an IEP must reflect not what the public agency can directly provide, but what the child needs.

For many reasons, it is recommended that a list of community resources be maintained and regularly updated by some member of the IEP team. Specialists in language development, reading, motor therapy, vision, speech and hearing, and counseling, for example, should be contacted in advance so that when a child's needs are being discussed and a recommendation is made, a referral can be appropriately planned.

Quite frequently local chapters of the Learning Disabilities Association of America (LDA) or other advocacy groups maintain such listings. It should be emphasized, however, that it is against the policies of LDA to endorse or recommend any school, therapy, professional, or system. A list of state offices of LDA may be obtained by writing to the national offices of LDA, 4156 Library Road, Pittsburgh, Pennsylvania 15234 (email: info@LDAAmerica.org). By writing to the main office in your own state, you can determine the location of your nearest chapter and request information you need.

The director of special education in your school district, or the office of the intermediate public agency (county school district offices) will quite frequently have the names and addresses of local representatives of the American Speech and Hearing Association, International Reading Association, and Council for Exceptional Children. Through such resources, contacts can be made for specialists with needed skills in a variety of areas related to the IEP.

Locally, the telephone book or internet can provide contact information for professional organizations such as the local medical association and optometric association. In addition, the local health department may have many services available.

Where the school is not prepared to offer a specific service, and a contact with an independent professional is necessary, a file of such services becomes an indispensable tool for the team.

12. **I.E.P. Revisions**. The new law requires that a child's IEP be reviewed periodically, not less than annually, to determine if the annual goals are being achieved. The IEP should be revised to address lack of expected progress, if this is the case, the results of reevaluation, information provided by the parents, the child's anticipated needs, or other relevant matters.

Writing a comprehensive educational program is no easy task.It takes time and care. Revising the program, if it becomes necessary, is just as challenging. There is no assurance that any student is going to remain with the same teacher, be mainstreamed, or be in a self-contained or part-day program in the following school year. Valuable time in a child's academic program is going to be saved, and wisely used, if the next professional does not have to waste valuable time learning how to work with that child.

If it is necessary, an IEP may be amended or revised during the year for which it was written. For any number of reasons, this may be necessary. The student may have lost considerable time at school because of illness; there may be emotional factors that were not as seriously considered initially as they should have been; there may have been a change of teachers; or the initial IEP was simply too ambitious or not ambitious enough. If there are amendments, the same steps as were initially used, must be used again. Amending an IEP should be carried out only on consultation with all those involved with the student.

In making changes to a child's IEP, the parent of a child with a disability and the LEA may agree not to convene an IEP meeting. Instead, the current IEP may be amended or modified. The changes may be made either by the entire IEP team or by amending the IEP rather than by redrafting the entire IEP. Not all members of the IEP team must be present for its amendment if the member's area of expertise is not involved and if the parent and LEA consent to the excusal.

XVI

Interviewing Parents and Students

Amid testing, reviewing records, obtaining releases for information, notifying parents and team members of meeting dates, and testing, the simple act of meeting with parents and with the student can be very easily overlooked. Yet, information obtained from such meetings can have dramatic implications on the shaping of the student's program. Whereas parents may feel intimidated in a large meeting, the opportunity to discuss the child's needs and background in a small, comfortable setting may yield facts and feelings that would otherwise go unnoticed.

In establishing a meeting time and place for an interview between a team member (probably the person who knows the family and the student best), and the parents and student, it should be made clear that this conference will precede the larger decision-making meeting and that it will be informal.

Depending on the age and specific learning and developmental needs of the student, a decision should be reached on whether parents and their child should come together or whether they should have separate conferences. In any case, it is wise to have sufficient time, perhaps an hour at the most, and to have a setting with no physical barriers such as a desk separating the parties.

Suggestions for making this an informative session include:

- Know the student well enough, from records, etc., so that time isn't wasted.

- Explain or re-state the purpose of the meeting.

- Explain the rights of the parents regarding the entire process of IEP preparation.

- Ask about health, hobbies, family interactions, interests, and other meaningful information.

- Indicate a respect for the family's values.

- Ask a few questions—allow the parents and/or student to talk with one another.

- If you are taking notes, indicate why you are doing it, and take as few as possible.

- Be a good listener.

- Talk about both short- and long-range goals.

- Avoid using complicated educational terms or unfamiliar acronyms.

Emphasize to parents and to the student that they are important members of the team and that their feelings, comments, suggestions, and needs are vital to success of the program.

XVII

Confidentiality of Information

In the interests of protecting both the student and the parent, the new law has established specific ways that the confidential nature of records will be maintained.

1. Parents must be informed of public agency policies regarding storage, disclosure to third parties, retention, and destruction of all information regarding their children.

2. Parents have the right to inspect and review any education records relating to their children which are collected, maintained, or used by the agency. Agencies must respond to this request without unnecessary delay and before any meeting regarding an IEP or hearing related to the identification, evaluation, or placement of the child, and in no case more than 45 days after the request has been made.

3. Parents have the right to reasonable response from the agency for explanations and interpretations of the records. In addition, parents have the right to have a representative of their choosing inspect and review these records, and the right to request that the agency provide copies of the records if failure to do so would effectively prevent the parents from exercising the right to inspect and review them.

4. Agencies may presume that the parent has authority to inspect and review these records unless the agency has been advised that the parent does not have that authority because, for example, of guardianship, separation matters, etc.

5. Agencies must maintain a record of parties obtaining

access to education records collected, maintained, or used (except access by parents and authorized employees of that agency) including the name of the party, the date access was given, and the purpose for which the party is authorized to use the records.

6. If records contain information on more than one child, parents have the right to inspect and review only the information relating to their own child or to be informed of that specific information.

7. Agencies must provide parents, on request, a list of the types and locations of education records collected, maintained, or used by the agency.

8. An agency may charge a fee for copies of records which are made for parents if the fee does not effectively prevent the parents from exercising their right to inspect and review those records. But no fee may be charged for searching or retrieving information.

9. Parents have the right to request that the agency which maintains records on their child, if they believe it to be inaccurate or misleading, or violates the privacy or other rights of the child, to amend that information. (The agency shall decide whether to amend the information within a reasonable time of receipt of the request. If the agency refuses, it must inform the parent and advise the parent of the right to a due process hearing.)

10. The consent of parents must be obtained before personally identifiable information is disclosed to anyone other than officials of participating agencies collecting or using that information, or when it is used for any purpose other than meeting a requirement of the law.

11. Each agency must appoint one official who will assume responsibility for ensuring confidentiality of personally identifiable records. In addition, all persons collecting or

using such information must receive training or instruction regarding the state's policies and procedures under the law, and each agency must maintain a list, for public inspection, of the names and positions of those employees within the agency who may have access to such records.

12. Agencies must inform parents when such information is no longer needed to provide educational services to the child. The information must be destroyed at the request of the parents. A permanent record of the student's name, address, and phone number, his or her grades, attendance record, classes attended, grade level completed, and year completed may be maintained without time limitation. Parents, however, should be advised that total destruction of all records, other than those indicated, might not be wise in terms of future needs of that student; for example, Social Security benefits, etc.

As a final note, states, under the new law, were advised to include policies and procedures regarding the extent to which children would be afforded rights of privacy similar to those afforded to parents, taking into consideration the age of the child and type or severity of disability. (Under the regulations for the Family Educational Rights and Privacy Act, the rights of parents regarding education records are transferred to the student at age 18.)

XVIII

Provisions for Inclusion

The law provides that, to the maximum extent appropriate, disabled children in both public and private settings be educated with children who are not disabled and that special classes, separate schooling, or other removal occur only when the nature or severity of the disability is such that education in regular classes with the use of supplementary aids and services cannot be achieved satisfactorily.

In planning the IEP, statements must be included that indicate where and how children will be included, where appropriate, in the mainstream, both during the school day and after school. The local education agency must ensure that each child with a disability participates with nondisabled children in those services and activities to the maximum extent appropriate to the needs of that child.

The following characteristics are indicators of fully inclusive programs for students with disabilities. They can serve as guidelines in planning for inclusion.

1. Students are members of chronologically age-appropriate general education classrooms in their normal schools of attendance.

2. Students move with peers to subsequent grades in school.

3. No special class exists except as a place for enrichment activities for all students.

4. Disability type or severity of disability does not preclude involvement in full inclusion programs.

5. The special education and general education teachers collaborate to ensure:

   a. the student's natural participation as a regular member of the class;

   b. the systematic instruction of the student's IEP objectives;

   c. the adaptation of core curriculum and/or materials to facilitate student participation and learning.

6. Research-based interventions are supported and encouraged in the general education classroom.

7. The staff to student ratio for an itinerant special education teacher is equivalent to the special class ratio, and aide support is at least the level it would be in a special class.

8. Supplemental instructional services (e.g., communication, mobility, adapted P.E.) are provided to students in classrooms and community settings through a transdisciplinary team approach.

9. Regularly scheduled collaborative planning meetings are held with general education staff, special education staff, parents and related-service staff in attendance as indicated, in order to support initial and ongoing program development and monitoring.

10. There is always a certificated employee (special education teacher, resource specialist, or other) assigned to supervise and assist any classified staff (e.g., paraprofessional) working with specific students in general education classrooms.

11. Special education students who are fully included are considered a part of the total class count for class size purposes. In other words, even when a student is not counted for general education ADA, the child is not an "extra" student

above the contractual class size.

12. General ability awareness is provided to staff, students and parents at the school site through formal or informal means, on an individualized basis. This is most effective when ability awareness is incorporated with general education curriculum.

13. Plans exist for transition of students to next classes and schools of attendance in inclusive situations.

In summary, all students are members of the general education classroom, with some students requiring varying levels of support from special education.

XIX

Due Process Procedures

One of the important safeguards built into the new law is the right of parents to request a fair hearing of their feelings should there be dissatisfaction with any matter relating to initiating or changing the identification, evaluation, or educational placement of their child, or the provision of a free and appropriate education for their child.

Either the parent or the public educational agency may initiate a hearing on referral or placement of the child. The hearing must be conducted by the state educational agency or the public agency directly responsible for the education of the child.

The public agency shall inform the parent of any free or low cost legal and other relevant services available in the area if the parent requests the information or the parent or the agency initiates a hearing. It has been found, however, that mediation before a hearing is formalized is the best way to settle many disputes that might arise.

A hearing officer is typically a qualified professional who is knowledgeable about the law. A hearing may not be conducted by any person who is an employee of the state or local education agency that is involved in the education or care of the child, or by any person having a personal or professional interest that would conflict with his or her objectivity in the hcaring. Being paid by the agency to conduct the hearing does not mean the hearing officer is an employee.

Any party to a hearing has the right to:

- be accompanied and advised by counsel or by individuals with special knowledge or training with respect to problems of disabled children

- present evidence and confront, cross-examine, and compel the attendance of witnesses

- obtain a written or electronic record of the hearing

- obtain written findings of facts and decisions

Parents involved in hearings must be given the right to have the child present and open the hearings to the public. A decision made in a hearing is final unless a party to the hearing appeals the decision if conducted by other than the state educational agency.

In this case, any party aggrieved by the findings and decision in the hearing may appeal to the state educational agency. The state, in this case, will impartially review the entire hearing record, ensure that the procedures were consistent with due process requirements, seek additional evidence if necessary, afford the parties an opportunity for oral or written argument, or both (at the discretion of the reviewing official), make an independent decision on completion of review, and give a copy of written findings and the decision to both parties. This decision is final unless a party brings civil action.

Under IDEA 2004, the school district or other public agency must convene a resolution meeting for issues that do not involve discipline. A resolution session is a new provision of the new law that provides an opportunity for parents and local educational agencies to resolve issues in an efficient and effective manner so that parents and school districts can avoid due process hearings and solve problems more quickly. Within 15 days of when a complaint is filed, the LEA must convene a resolution session between the parents and the relevant members of the IEP team. The parties have the option of waiving the meeting or participating in in mediation instead of a resolution meeting.

If the parents request the hearing, the meeting must occur

within 15 days of when the district or other public agency receives the due process hearing request. If the parties are unable to resolve the dispute through the resolution meeting within 30 days of receipt of the hearing request, the due process hearing timeline begins. Unless the timelines are extended at the request of one of the parties, due process hearings must be held and a final decision issued within 45 calendar days following the end of the resolution period. A copy of the decision must be provided to each of the parties.

Since the federal law presents the basic outline or format for states, states have the right to make additions to the law which are suitable in their own states. The federal outline, however, may not be altered. It can only be improved upon and enhanced. For this reason, it is recommended that anyone involved under the regulations of IDEA, including parents, obtain a copy of their own state guidelines from the state office of special education, state capitol, or through their local, state legislative representative.

Checklist Regarding Parent Rights

Any factor not complied with could affect the results of all proceedings and determinations regarding programming for the child.

1. Have parents been notified in advance of their rights?

2. Have parents been notified of all meetings dealing with identification, evaluation, and educational placement in advance?

3. Have communications been in the native tongue of the parents?

4. Have all communications been clear and understandable?

5. Has a record been maintained of all telephone calls, home visits, and copies of notes and letters?

6. Have meetings been set up at a time that is convenient to the parents?

7. Have results, written documents, and discussions been written in a way that is understandable to the parents as opposed to appearing in highly technical language?

8. Have parents been notified that they may bring others to meetings to assist them?

9. Have parents been notified that the child may be invited to all meetings that are of concern to him/her if it is appropriate?

10. Have parents been notified of their rights to have an outside evaluation, paid for by the local agency, if they disagree with the findings of the assessment committee?

11. Has a written summary been provided for parents of all meetings pertaining to their child's program?

12. If parents have not responded to notes, letters, telephone calls, or home visits, has someone or some committee member been appointed to act in place of the parent?

13. Have parents been notified of their rights regarding confidentiality of all records dealing with their child?

14. Has an interpreter been present at meetings when language might be a problem?

15. Have parents been notified of their rights regarding impartial due process procedures should there be dissatisfaction with committee conclusions?

16. Have parents signed and dated all documents regarding decisions reached regarding their child's progress?

17. If parents cannot attend any meetings, has a signed waiver been secured from them indicating they have been contacted but cannot attend?

18. Are the parents aware of their rights regarding the privacy and confidentiality of all records pertaining to their child?

19. Have parents been advised to maintain their own record of meetings, contracts, and dates?

XX

Early Intervention Services

IDEA establishes important rights and essential services to young children with disabilities, ages birth through five years, and their families. Part C of IDEA governs the early intervention program for infants and toddlers, ages birth through two years.

The term "infants and toddlers with disabilities" means individuals under three years of age who need early intervention services because they are experiencing developmental delays, as measured by appropriate diagnostic instruments and procedures in one or more of the areas of cognitive development, physical development, communication development, social or emotional development, and adaptive development; or has a diagnosed physical or mental condition that has a high probability of resulting in developmental delay. Early intervention services are intended to meet the needs of the child in physical development, cognitive development, communication development, social or emotional development, or adaptive development.

The purpose of IDEA, Part C, as defined by Congress is:

1. To enhance the development of infants and toddlers with disabilities and to minimize their potential delay and to recognize the significant brain development that occurs during a child's first three years of life

2. To reduce educational costs by minimizing the need for special education and related services after infants and toddlers with disabilities reach school age

3. To maximize the potential for their independent living in our society

4. To enhance the capacity of families to meet the special needs of infants and toddlers

5. To enhance the capacity of state and local agencies and service providers to identify, evaluate, and meet the needs of all children, particularly minority, low-income, inner-city, and rural children, and infants and toddlers in foster care

In order to accomplish this purpose, the federal government provides financial assistance to the states so they can "develop and implement a statewide, comprehensive, coordinated, multi-disciplinary, interagency system that provides early intervention services for infants and toddlers with disabilities and their families."

Early intervention services are provided under public supervision by qualified personnel in natural environments. There is no cost to the families, except where federal or state law provides for a system of payments by families, including a schedule of sliding fees. The services include:

- family training, counseling, and home visits

- special instruction

- speech-language pathology and audiology services, and sign language and cued language services

- occupational therapy

- physical therapy

- psychological services

- service coordination services

- medical services for diagnostic or evaluation purposes

- early identification, screening, and assessment services

- health services necessary to enable the infant or toddler

to benefit from the other early intervention services

- social work services

- vision services

- assistive technology devices and assistive technology services

- transportation and related costs that are necessary to enable an infant or toddler and family to receive another service

XXI

Transition Services

Transition services are coordinated activities that are focused on improving academic achievement and functional performance in order to facilitate the disabled child's movement from school to the post-school setting. The post-school setting includes post-secondary education, vocational education, integrated employment (including supported employment), continuing and adult education, adult services, independent living, or community participation.

As is the case with other aspects of the IEP, transition services must be based on the individual child's needs, strengths, preferences, and interests. The services may include instruction, related services, community experiences, and the development of employment and other post-school adult living objectives. In some circumstances, the transition activities will focus on the acquisition of daily living skills and functional vocational evaluation. Beginning not later than the first IEP that takes effect when the child is 16, appropriate post-secondary goals and the transition services needed to reach them must be included.

Awareness of post-secondary opportunities should be viewed as a long-range process and should begin as early as possible, even if they are not stated directly in the IEP. Career awareness and the development of work attitudes may begin within the elementary years. Career exploration of specific vocational areas and behaviors often occurs at the junior high level and continues throughout the four years of high school. Structured training experiences such as community classrooms and work experience generally begin between the ages of 13 to 16. Career placement should certainly begin to be addressed during the two years prior to leaving school. Such activities will help students with disabilities gain an accurate understanding of the job market. Technology, legislation, and the example of successful disabled adults have resulted in a wide range of opportunities in the economy. The transition services provided to disabled students should help them make career choices based on their interests and abilities, not to simply accept whatever they think is available.

Vocational education services can be included within the IEP in several ways. Depending on the age and ability level of the student, goals for instruction can be included in the area of grooming skills, social skills training, and general work behaviors. As the student moves toward secondary school age, vocational education services should be included in the IEP through training experiences in the classroom and the community. For example, experiences may include travel training on routes within a student's daily schedule and training on specific work tasks in the classroom and at sites throughout the community, such as local businesses or industries.

A document called a "summary of performance" is now required by IDEA 2004 for students who graduate from secondary school with a regular diploma or exceed the age eligibility for a free appropriate public education. The summary of performance must include information on the student's academic achievement and functional performance. In addition, it should include recommendations on how to assist the student in meeting postsecondary goals. The intention of the summary is to provide useful and understandable information to the student with a disability, the family, and any agency, including postsecondary schools, that may provide services to the student upon transition. It is important to note that a new evaluation is not necessary.

XXII

Private School Placement

Under some circumstances, a child with a disability may be placed in a private school. This may be the case if the local education agency is unable to provide a free appropriate public education for the child.

If placement in a private or public residential program is necessary so that special education and related services can be provided to the disabled child, the program, including non-medical care and room and board, must be at no cost to the parents of that child. An IEP must be developed and implemented for that child before placement.

A representative of the private school must attend the IEP team meeting. If this is not possible, for example, because of distance, other methods such as conferences or phone calls should be used. The agency must also develop an IEP on each disabled child in a private school if placement occurred prior to the date the new law became effective.

After a child enters a private school, any meetings to review and revise the IEP may be initiated and conducted by that school or facility at the discretion of the public agency. In such meetings, however, it is the responsibility of the public agency to ensure that the parents and an agency representative are involved in any decisions regarding the IEP and that they agree to proposed changes before they are implemented. In short, the IEP process is similar to that for children in public schools.

There must be no cost to parents, when their child has been placed by a public agency in a private school. But that school must meet state and local educational standards. In addition, the public agency must ensure that the child has all the rights of a disabled child who is served by a public agency.

If, on the other hand, a disabled child has available a free appropriate public education and the parents choose to place their child in a private school, the public agency is not required to pay for the child's education at the private school. Disagreements concerning public or private placement are subject to due process procedures. If this is the case, the child is still eligible for special education and related services. This may include dual enrollment or public school personnel serving within the private school if the child's needs are not being met by services normally provided at the private school.

The decision to place a child in a private educational setting is one that must be carefully considered in light of many factors. The major question to be answered is that of advantages and disadvantages as they affect the total needs of the student. This can only be answered once the IEP is put together, either in a preliminary or completed form, since the IEP reflects those social, emotional, learning, vocational, and therapeutic needs. It is important to always remember that the IEP is a statement of the student's needs, not a statement of what resources the public agency has immediately available.

XXIII

Specific Learning Disabilities

Because so many children who are classified as learning disabled are affected by IDEA, a few words need to be said about this condition.

The law defines a "specific learning disability" as: A disorder in one or more of the basic psychological processes involved in understanding or in using language, spoken or written, which may manifest itself in an imperfect ability to listen, think, speak, read, write, spell, or to do mathematical calculations. The term includes such conditions as perceptual disabilities, brain injury, minimal brain dysfunction, dyslexia, and developmental aphasia. The term does not include children who have learning problems which are primarily the result of visual, hearing, or motor disabilities, of mental retardation, of emotional disturbance, or of environmental, cultural, or economic disadvantage.

As was mentioned earlier, an important change in the identification of children with specific learning disabilities has been included in the new law. The traditional discrepancy between achievement and intellectual ability in reading, listening, speaking, or mathematics may still be used, but a second approach, response to intervention (RTI), is also allowed by the law. Sometimes called responsiveness to intervention, the approach is a multi-stage technique based on how well students respond to instructional practices.

Before determining that a child has a specific learning disability, the evaluation team should consider whether the child received appropriate high-quality, research-based instruction in regular education settings. Moreover, the results of repeated assessments of achievement during instruction must havebeen provided to the child's parents. If the child has not made adequate progress under the conditions specified after a reasonable period of time, the child should be referred for an evaluation to determine if special education and related services are needed.

In evaluating a child suspected of having a specific learning disability, the team should be collectively qualified to conduct an appropriate individual diagnostic assessment in the areas of speech and language, academic achievement, intellectual development, and social-emotional development. It should include a special education teacher, the child's general education teacher (if the child does not have a regular teacher, a regular classroom teacher qualified to teach a child of his or her age, or, for a child of less than school age, an individual qualified by the state educational agency to teach a child of his or her age), and other professionals, if appropriate, such as a school psychologist, reading teacher, or educational therapist.

At least one qualified team member, other than the child's regular teacher, shall observe the child's academic performance in the regular setting. In the case of a child of less than school age or out of school, a team member shall observe the child in an environment appropriate for a child of that age.

A team may determine that a child has a specific learning disability if the child does not achieve commensurate with his or her age and ability levels in one or more of the areas that appear on the list on the following page. As part of the determination, the team must consider whether the child was provided with learning experiences appropriate for the child's age and ability levels. A learning disability would be present if the team finds that a child has a severe discrepancy between achievement and intellectual potential in one or more of the following areas:

132

- oral expression
- listening comprehension
- written expression
- basic reading skill
- reading comprehension
- mathematical calculation
- mathematical problem solving

The team may not identify a child as having a specific learning disability if the severe discrepancy between ability and achievement is primarily the result of:

- visual, hearing, or motor disability
- mental retardation
- emotional disturbance
- environmental, cultural, or economic disadvantage

The team shall prepare a written report of the results of the evaluation, which must include a statement of:

- whether the child has a specific learning disability
- the basis for making this determination
- the relevant behavior noted during the observation of the child and the relationship of the behavior to the child's academic functioning
- the educationally relevant medical findings, if any
- whether the child does not achieve commensurate with the child's age
- whether there are strengths and weaknesses in performance, achievement, or both relative to intel-

lectual development

- instructional strategies used and the student-centered data collected in response to scientific, research-based intervention

In addition, each team member shall certify in writing whether the report reflects his or her conclusion. If it does not reflect his or her conclusion, the team member must submit a separate statement presenting his or her conclusions.

There may be additions to the basic federal law, as outlined above. In such cases, it is important to review the specifics of the plan in your own state.

XXIV

Interests and Learning Characteristics

Because disabled individuals often learn differently from their nondisabled peers, the ways they are taught must correspond to their characteristics and interests. The examples below demonstrate how this can be accomplished.

"Luke," age 12, had a history of behavioral and learning problems since preschool. In spite of the fact that he was placed in a special learning class at age six, part day (a resource room), for reading, spelling, and mathematics, the kinds of progress expected were simply not forthcoming. He had a supportive family, caring teachers, and all kinds of back-up services. But the appropriate thrust for his program could not be pinpointed.

Luke had perceptual difficulties, particularly visual, and eye tracking problems (but no need for corrective lenses). He was hyperactive, and had a measured IQ of 124.

Luke, when offered free time, always drew. It had been noted throughout his educational records, "Luke draws too much," "Luke should not spend so much time drawing," "Luke loves to draw," and so on. A sixth grade creative resource teacher, "Sarah Jones," made an enormous positive step by considering Luke's art interest. Looking for a way to reach Luke, she discovered that the one element that ran through all of his recorded school history was drawing. This was his major interest, one he had sustained for many years. Water colors, charcoal, pastels, crayons, pen and pencil; whatever it was, Luke drew.

Mrs. Jones revised the IEP for Luke. It was acceptable to his parents. They were as supportive as they had been in the past. Luke's spelling, handwriting, and mathematics were all to be based on drawing. Measuring lines, laying out house plans, designing skyscrapers, drawing instead of comprehension checks, designing cursive handwriting styles—all this and much more—revived an interest in school and learning for a youngster whose future was not promising.

"Carla" was a secondary school student with a history of behavioral problems. It was never really quite clear whether she had a true learning disability. Results of tests and teacher reports suggested that she might have one. But her behavior was so disruptive that she was thought of as a "gang leader" at school and in the community. She was, as in so many other cases, placed in a resource room setting because it was felt that it would remove her from the regular classroom where she played havoc with teachers, and she could get some small group assistance, to which, incidentally, she did not respond.

It took one observant teacher to notice over a period of several months, that, in spite of Carla's unique behaviors, she had a flair for jewelry and clothes, many that she made herself. That one clue was Carla's salvation. The teacher, serving part time as a job counselor, spoke with Carla, affirmed her hunches that there might be a vocational link buried somewhere in clothes, and got Carla an after-school job in a women's apparel shop.

Suddenly, a new world opened up for Carla. Writing sales slips required legible handwriting and spelling, reading tags on apparel meant applying reading skills, talking with patrons meant improvements in communication skills, and, certainly, using the cash register meant sharpening her math skills. Today, some years later, Carla operates her own dress shop and employs four women. The clue: Carla's interest in clothes. It turned her around.

The point of these examples is to point out that determining an interest in a special-needs child offers a platform for remedial and academic action. One way, obviously, as the story of Luke points out, is that of observation.

Another way is to ask the child what he or she likes to do with free time, on weekends, on holidays; what are favorite television programs; who best friends are; what is done with best friends; who are adults he or she would like to be like. Talk to parents and see what they have to say about hobbies, best friends, and free time. And, yes, talk with previous teachers to see what you can identify as take-off points.

What you may find out is that Eloise has an abiding interest in rocket ships or that Jake is fascinated with camping and the outdoors. These are important leads because you can direct your search for materials so that they correspond to where that specific child is functioning.

Sadly, the whole matter of interests in children with special learning needs is quite often ignored or overlooked in the long-term process of skill development. It is true that children with disabilities need direct instruction in critical skill areas, the effort devoted to identifying their interests almost always pays off.

Because children grow and develop, and their range of understanding of their own personal world changes, do an interest inventory at least once a year, even if it is informal. Modify the approach, when it is deemed timely, in the types of materials being used with that student.

Learning Characteristics

In addition to becoming familiar with a child's interests, teachers and others should determine how the child learns. There has been considerable discussion over the years on the value of assessment to pinpoint needs in reading achievement, spelling competency, mathematics competency, and handwriting abilities, but little discussion at the grass roots level of which styles are preferred by specific learners.

For example, while the majority of children become visual learners, this is not true of many disabled children. Their visual systems, quite often, are in such disarray that while they may function adequately out of school at far-point tasks, near-point learning styles are frustrating, demanding, and challenging. Conversely, some disabled children are excellent visual learners, but unless some kind of assessment or observation is carried out, this would never be known.

Knowing the primary modality channel and other learning characteristics allows teachers to capitalize on the child's strengths. Exploration into learning styles requires some deliberation on the part of the teacher. For example, perhaps comprehension should be reinforced by having manipulatives (wooden blocks, thread spools, etc.) available to the child. Perhaps rather than near-point writing on standard-size paper, the child should write on the chalkboard; perhaps the child should carry a recorder (or have one available at school) for recording lectures. These are important factors in the IEP process. Why?

Earlier in this text, the IEP was compared to taking a trip. One needs a goal, a proposed route, and a way of knowing when the destination has been reached. It is surprising to see IEPs that list goals and objectives but do not state the "how" part of the process. How is one going to guide the child to the destination? The only sensible way to lay out a program, the "how" part of the IEP, is to know how the student best learns.

One of the least understood characteristics of children with disabilities is *when* they learn best. Researchers have begun looking at the time-dependent learning patterns of general education students. There is little research on when children with a disability learn best. Based on research and self reports from general education students, there is probably no predictable pattern. This being the case, it is worth investigating through observation and easily quantified behaviors such as time on task, behavior incidents, and preferred activities when a child seems to learn best and what activities best match the child's temporal pattern. Keep in mind that it is probably inappropriate to make generalizations about the behavior patterns of children with disabilities without a significant research basis. Moreover, factors such as discipline must be considered. A child may, for example, be more alert and thus "teachable" in the early afternoon, but the child may also be prone to behavioral problems at the same time. Like other learning characteristics, it is necessary to learn about the child before making decisions about instruction and related activities.

Determining a child's learning characteristics is not easy but it certainly pays big dividends in meeting the goals and objectives laid out in the child's IEP. Here are some questions you can ask the student. You can vary the wording to match the age and developmental level of the student. In addition, the teacher, parent, or other adult familiar with the student may suggest additional questions.

1. What time do you go to bed?

2. Do you bounce out of bed or take a long time to really wake up?

3. Do you find that it helps to take notes in class?

4. Do you use a tape recorder to review what your teacher says?

5. Do you like to repair things?

6. Do you like to draw?

7. Do you think you are better in classes where there is discussion rather than reading?

8. Do you find you learn more when someone is reading to you?

9. Do you have favorite foods? What are they?

10. Does it help you to draw a picture of a math problem before you start to solve it (or figure it out)?

11. Do you like to work on the same project for a long time or do a little bit at a time?

12. Do you like to check your work before you turn it in or want to turn it in as soon as it is finished?

13. Does it help if you "talk" your way through an assignment before you start or do you like to just it without planning?

14. Do you work better alone or in a group?

15. When you think that an assignment is difficult, what do you do?

Obviously, in any questions that are asked of the student, one must be careful not to violate the principle of invasion of personal privacy. It will be helpful to repeat the process at least once a year. Determine whether there have been any dramatic changes. Then compare the results with corresponding changes in academic performance.

XXV

Self-Esteem

There has been a considerable recognition in recent years about the need in low-achieving students for the development of the concept of "I'm really OK." What has become clear to parents and educators is that self-esteem rightfully deserves a place in the IEP.

Teachers in special education have long believed that students begin to feel better about themselves when small steps are laid out and successfully mastered. For example, "Look, Tonie, first of all we're going to work on having you be able to write your first and last name in cursive. OK?" This is a short-term goal even though it may take four weeks.

After four weeks, Tonie is able to successfully write, in cursive and legibly, her full name. Then comes objective two. "Now, Tonie, we're going to work on having you write not only your name, but your full address, city, and state, with the zip code. Let's say you want to write for something you see advertised in a magazine or newspaper. Or, let's say that you are going to apply for a part-time job somewhere. You'll need to be able to write this information."

The pattern here is that Tonie is being given small objectives that will lead to success. As her performance improves, her sclf-esteem goes up.

Here is another way to approach the goal of having the student learn functional cursive writing. Suppose that in the interest inventory, Rick expressed a great deal of interest in car repair. Why not, then, have him learn the names of car parts and use them for cursive writing. Rick may well have a "wish list" of automobile tools he would like to own. Or he might wish to create a list of high performance cars. The point is that the goal or objective need not change. It is the way in which it is carried out that will vary from one student to another.

Many students with disabilities feel frustrated with their low achievement levels. This is why breaking tasks into small, manageable components that they can master relatively quickly leads to a success-oriented program.

This is where the family must cooperate and be aware of the objectives and goals being laid out for Tonie. Subtle, indiscreet comments can easily be made in a family setting, things that undermine the development of self-esteem. It is often not uncommon for a family member to say, "Oh, don't let Gina do that. She's a little awkward, you know, and she has a learning disability." Comments like these only serve to diminish Gina's willingness to take chances and risk failure in order to learn.

Self-esteem and perceived relevancy are closely related. "Spike" was an eleventh grade student who had had a phenomenal history of failure throughout his school years. Not only were his reading skills quite low, but his performance in spelling, handwriting, history, math, and other subjects was abysmal. No one could seem to reach Spike. No amount of encouragement seemed to have any effect on school achievement. He had lost all interest in school. Even the fact that he showed up for school was somewhat astounding in light of his many problems. But one thing he was not was a behavior problem. That, perhaps, was his saving grace.

Out of the blue, the school received a call from a neighborhood merchant. It was November, and he was setting up his Christmas tree lot. Could the school recommend five students who would be reliable and honest? Spike was recommended by one of the staff. One of the issues that was raised was whether he could make change when people paid for their trees. Well, another staff member commented, yes, he probably could.

Spike went for a briefing at the lot and was excited with the prospects of making a decent hourly rate. When he returned to school, he told his counselor that, in addition to the hourly pay, he would receive an additional incentive bonus of five percent for each tree he sold. What was this "'five percent" all about, he wondered.

For the first time in his life, fractions and percentages took on a new meaning. Spike suddenly understood that he would pocket five cents out of each dollar for each tree sold. What an incentive to hustle! But what was amazing was Spike's new-found interest in the fact that math made sense for everyday living. And Spike's self-esteem shot up enormously when he turned out to be the top seller at the lot. In his case, there was a turn-around because of the relevancy of making money.

Much has been written on self-esteem. There is no need to repeat it here. The point is, when self-esteem is perceived to be low, it should be one of the goals and objectives of an IEP and should deserve the same attention as do other aspects of a formal learning program. This is especially true when students are 16 or older and are planning to make the transition to a postsecondary setting. Self-esteem is enormously important in both employment and postsecondary education, so it certainly should be included in the IEP of older students.

XXVI

Socialization and Other Factors

The determination of a disability and the development of an IEP are based on assessments and observations of more than academic achievement. The social and emotional development of the child must also be considered.

It is not unusual, for example, to pinpoint children who have real needs in socialization, or students who have unique talents, for example, in art or music, or students who may have substance abuse problems, or children who have what appears to be nutritional deficits, or children who need assistance in being better groomed. When legislation requiring an IEP was first passed, the numbers of single-parent families and the number of working mothers was far less than it is now. Parents are beset with problems that can draw their attention away from the special needs youngster. Situations frequently occur in which teachers and special education staff are disappointed when the homework they send home with the child is either never returned or never completed. Or they are annoyed that there is virtually no carryover at home of recommendations made by the special education staff. What these personnel do not explore are the conditions in the home setting. One working mother said, "What am I supposed to do? I get home at 6:00, frayed from traffic. I have to put dinner on the table. My kids are dead tired and go to bed at 8:30. When is there any time to supervise homework? I'm too busy to do all of this."

Talking with the parent or parents can reveal some fascinating information. All teachers know the value of modeling behavior. But it is not uncommon to have anxious parents, deeply concerned about their child's needs in reading, for example, to seldom sit as a family for supper and talk before rushing to the television set, or never reading a book in front of their children, much less a newspaper or anything else.

With respect to substance abuse, there are personnel within a school district and resources in the community for assisting families when the possibilities exist that there are drugs being used. As for the possibility of child abuse or child molestation, this must be reported immediately to school district administrators if there is any question from remarks the child makes that either of these is going on.

Socialization

Parents are understandably upset when their young child becomes a "Nobody will play with me" loner. And clearly these feelings of hurt and anger are compounded when the youngster reaches the teen years. There's something terribly poignant about a teenager who isn't invited to a neighborhood swim party, or a prom, or something as simple as a trip to the movies with a few friends.

The feeling grows worse because the parents typically feel helpless and incompetent in the face of this rejection. And chances are great that these feelings cannot be shared with the teenager, who may already have begun to engage in who-cares attitude, saying "I don't care—I didn't want to go anyway."

When learning disabilities were first identified as a valid disabling condition, parents—and educators, too—put all of their eggs in the education basket. "If only we can teach the child to read and write and compute," they said, "everything will work out." And so massive remedial programs were launched, many of which did teach the LD youngster to read and write and compute.

And yet, as the years unfolded, it became abundantly clear that mastery of academics was not the total answer, that there was still a piece of the puzzle missing, and it was the critically important component–social skills. Here were youngsters who may indeed have achieved a modicum of academic success but who nevertheless could not be considered "educated" in terms of peer and other relationships, who were not ready for the job market because of their inability to relate well to others. Other categories of disabled students also face the same challenges.

Where to Start

It is safe to assume that many students with a disability, especially one that affects cognitive functioning, have no idea of what they are doing (or not doing) that is wrong, that "turns people off." They cannot judge their impact on others. The first step, then, is to make these young people aware. The teacher can help with this to some extent, but a parent, other adult in the family, or other family members will be the principal sources of modeling.

It will take some advance preparation, soul searching, and thought. Schedule a time for a quiet chat, haul out the milk and cookies or other snack, summon up your courage, and jump in! Parents know their own children, so they'll know best what to say. Here is a suggestion that has worked well for others that you may be able to adapt to your needs: "I thought we would talk about making friends and getting along with people. I don't mean the family—you do just fine with all of us at home. That's partly because we all know one another so well, and also because we don't constantly have to be on our best behavior with other family members. It's different with outsiders—they are usually quick to judge us by how we look and how we act—and so we have to think twice about what we say and do. I thought that you and I might talk about a few of these things and maybe even practice some of the situations you'll encounter outside of the family." Such a discussion assumes greater importance for disabled children in high school.

Conversation

Disabled students who are having problems with social skills typically err in one of two ways in conversation. Either they clam up and have little to say, or they talk too much on a topic that holds little interest for others. These students must learn the give-and-take of good conversation, and roleplaying is an effective way to do this. It is important that these students learn:

- the difference between a casual and an intimate conversation;
- the significance of facial expressions and body language;
- the amount of space they should leave between themselves and others;
- how to attend and respond to what the other person is saying and how to express this interest with questions;
- when and when not to speak of personal matters;
- the inappropriateness of foul language;
- how to interpret when the other person is bored and ready to terminate the conversation;
- how to pay and accept a sincere compliment;
- the discourtesy of interrupting;
- how to terminate a conversation;
- the difference between humor and sarcasm.

(Some of the aspects listed above will be explained in greater detail in the material that follows.)

Body Language and Facial Expression

A few basic principles cover areas that seem trivial but are very important.

1. Some learning disabled individuals stand too close—literally nose to nose—to the person with whom they are conversing, causing that person a degree of discomfort. Conversely, although not so often, they stand too far away. A comfortable distance for most people is arm's length.

2. Slumping in a chair and/or fiddling with an object signifies lack of attention, if not downright discourtesy, to others.

3. Arms folded across the chest can indicate a negative attitude.

4. Eye contact is important because it implies attentiveness and sincerity. (Also, someone who is telling an untruth has difficulty maintaining eye contact.)

5. Nodding the head affirmatively as the speaker talks conveys the reinforcing message that one is in agreement with what is being said.

6. A smile is a pleasant thing to witness, but one grows wary if the smile is constant, if the expression never varies.

7. The importance of a firm handshake for both boys and girls cannot be over-estimated.

8. Laughter should be used appropriately. Incessant giggling can be a distancing phenomenon.

Let's Not Get Personal!

Young people with a hidden disability often wonder if they should mention it to others. This is a difficult question to answer, particularly for learning disabled youngsters. Perhaps the most helpful answer is, "Yes, if it matters." In other words, it isn't necessary to share such information with the stranger sitting next to you on a bus for a short ride. It's a different

149

story with the people who live next door (who may have been puzzled and will be more accepting once they are aware of the problem). And, most important of all, is walking that fine line between using a disability as an excuse rather than as a reasonable explanation.

Some do's and don'ts for the teenager:

1. Feel free to compliment someone on his/her looks or dress. (Keep it light—not too effusive.) Never, never make a negative comment in a group, for example, "You've got a spot on your blouse." Such things are better mentioned in a way that is helpful and not embarrassing.

2. Don't discuss financial matters. It really isn't any of your business how much something costs or how much salary someone is paid.

3. If someone declines an invitation or can't speak on the telephone, don't ask why. Just say, "Okay, I'll ask (or call) you again." Don't criticize one member of a family to another—or one good friend to another. Don't ask the age of anyone over 21!

Creating Social Situations

The home can be an effective classroom for teaching social skills. It may take some extra work and planning, but the effort will produce positive results.

1. Invite guests for mealtime—any age will do—and then watch the teenager in action, both in terms of manners and conversation. Never criticize or correct the child when guests are present, but take mental notes and discuss them with the child later, keeping your approach positive. The following suggestions might be helpful: "It's more polite to ask someone to pass the butter than reaching across the table for it" or "You might want to try to keep your voice a little softer at the table." Often poor social skills that may

pass unnoticed by the family are more clearly seen when guests are present.

2. When you go to the movies or theatre, allow the teenager to buy the tickets and/or refreshments in order to learn about this procedure.

3. Eating in restaurants is a large part of social life. Provide plenty of experience with menus, tips, etc.

4. Make your home an open friendly place. The teenager will absorb some social skills simply by being around others even though they may be friends of siblings or parents. And certainly assure youngsters that their home is open to anyone they may wish to invite. (You may want to set certain rules about advance notification for mealtime guests.)

5. Check out clubs and social groups—the local Y, square dancing groups, hiking clubs, and so on—that offer something for the whole family so that you can provide a measure of protection until your teenager can go it alone.

6. Teach the teenager to play "social" games like chess, checkers, backgammon, ping pong, or others. Games like these are important for building friendships and for learning how to interact with others. They are far superior for these purposes than computer games, even those that involve online competition.

7. Broaden the youngsters' horizons any way you can, such as visiting museums, attending concerts or exhibits, and traveling. All such experiences will add to to their confidence and general knowledge.

8. Provide opportunities to use the public transportation system in your community.

You will probably find that there will be failures along the way, but there will be success, too. The best thing about teaching social skills is that you are sharing knowledge that you already have, and you can count on seeing improvement. Perhaps it will be slow, just one small step at a time, but it *will* come.

Most important of all, research suggests that there is a relationship between social skills and academic achievement even among young students. For this reason, social skills instruction and intervention are increasingly being recommended for children with disabilities and included in their IEPs.

XXVII

Advising Parents on Safeguarding Valuable Papers

Virtually every parent of a child who has been in a special program, public or private, as well as parents who have provided outside remedial services for their youngsters, has a drawer full of records and documents. When one is needed, for example, in an IEP meeting, it becomes a matter of scrambling through sheaves of papers to locate it.

Clearly, parents do not need anyone to point out the importance of saving and safeguarding every report and record on their children. Not only do these reports have great significance in the immediate future, but they may also be of importance in the post-school years when the youngster may be seeking rehabilitation, career training services, or on-the-job training.

The records and documents are already there. What may be helpful are some tips on organizing them. The suggestions that follow have come from both teachers and parents who have experienced the annoyance of not being able to locate a pertinent piece of information.

The first step is to purchase an accordion-type folder with at least ten pockets. Label each pocket and keep the folder in a convenient and safe place. As material is received, file it in the folder. Make sure that on dated material, the year is included. Often parents have experienced difficulty with recall when only the month and day were given on a report and the year wasn't. This can happen even on official documents from time to time.

The pockets might include the following:

1. **Official Records.**
   This would include birth certificates, Social Security card, diplomas, certificates of all kinds. Perhaps the single most important piece of information in this pocket would be a set of your child's fingerprints. Because of an epidemic of missing children, police and sheriff departments throughout the country have launched a free fingerprinting program. Generally, they will fingerprint children from infancy through age 16, although infants may have to be fingerprinted again later on for better prints. The fingerprints are given to parents for safekeeping.

2. **Report Cards.**
   This would include report cards from every school for each grade or level and might include other informal reports and comments from the school.

3. **Correspondence.**
   This would include not only copies of all correspondence received but also letters written about the child by the parent.

4. **Telephone Conversations**
   This would include a record (date and substance) of telephone conversations held with a professional about the child. This is of critical importance because telephone conversations have a way of fading fast. If there is not time to write down the substance immediately, perhaps a few salient points can be put on tape and transcribed later. The record of the call might also include a kind of dated log showing who was contacted, was call returned, if so, when, etc.

5. **Medical (including Neurological) Test Reports**.
   Immunization records as well as other records about illnesses can be included in this pocket. (Did Jane ever have three-day measles? When?)

6. **Psychological Test Reports**.
Generally, after psychological testing has been done, a conference is held between parent and professional. What is said during this conference can be fully as important as the test results. Take notes and keep them in this pocket.

7. **Visual and/or Auditory Test Reports**. (See #6 above)

8. **Work Samples.**
Samples of the child's school work should be kept beginning in preschool or kindergarten, always carefully dated. These are not only important developmental records but are great fun to savor as the years pass by.

9. **Photographs**.
Whenever possible, an annual photograph should be included. School photos are perfect for this pocket, but family snapshots will also serve.

10. **Out-of-Pocket**.
Whenever you must pull a piece of information from the folder, make sure that you record not only what piece of information was pulled, but when and to whom it was given. The folder can contain a pad and pencil on which to record removal and return of important documents.

In this day and age of instantly accessible photocopiers, it seems obvious that duplicates or triplicates of important documents should be made. Then, if one should be lost or mislaid, as frequently happens, a copy is instantly available.

Include a master sheet (also with extra photocopies) on which you can record the schools (and even camps) your child has attended from grade to grade, year to year, as well as the names of teachers, counselors, and principals, with their addresses when possible. You may feel that you'll never forget a certain teacher or principal, for example, but memories tend to grow dim after a few years. Record it all!

Keep the accordion folder in a safe place. Fireproof boxes are available at hardware stores. Their use is strongly recommended for these and other important family papers. And just in case you might be unavailable, let another family member know about these records and where you keep them. You might even want to let the child know. It can be encouraging to know that one's school work, report cards, photographs, etc., are kept in a very special place.

To supplement the file, some parents have found it not only helpful but enjoyable to keep a kind of diary of important developmental milestones—the first step, the first word, when the child was able to feed himself, when toilet training was accomplished. This information may prove useful during a child's evaluation and in developing the IEP.

Other Valuable Papers

A parent of a child diagnosed with a disability has the right to place all justified expenses in the medical deduction section of the annual income tax forms. Recent court cases have determined that a child may be diagnosed by a medical doctor or by a certified/licensed (adhering to state regulations) psychologist.

If a school or remedial service plainly indicates in its promotional literature (brochures, etc.) that it has qualified/certified teachers and that it is established to meet the needs of a specific group of disabled students, then deductions may be made for the school or service. These include travel expenses, tuition fees, equipment necessary to alleviate the condition, and so on.

For this reason, parents should be sure to keep records of diagnostic evaluations. Specifically, information should be retained that indicates clearly who did the evaluation and that person's license or certification information. This may be a state licensing number.

When recording expenses, retain invoices, dates (remember, as mentioned earlier, years are important—not just day and month), to whom payment was made, and for what reason. In short, this type of expense must be justified.

Keeping careful track of records and documents is one of the most important contributions that a parent can make to the long-range welfare of the child. Is it part of the IEP process? You bet it is! Professionals will respond positively to the parent who can immediately provide background material for the lengthy, detailed patient/client history forms that seem to be demanded in each new academic and/or clinical setting. Not only will the material be easily accessible, but it will be undeniably accurate. Such records, particularly when they can be lost or misplaced in a school setting, public or private, may easily affect the granting of S.S.I. monies, work training programs, or proof of a disability later in life.

Glossary of Basic Terms in Learning

abstract thinking: ability to think in terms of ideas.

ADD or **ADHD**: attention deficit disorder or attention deficit (hyperactivity) disorder.

agnosia: inability to interpret sensory impressions.

agraphia: inability to write words.

ambidexterity: complete efficiency in both right and left hands.

aphasia: defect or loss of the power of expression by speech, writing, or signs; or loss of comprehension of spoken or written language due to injury or disease of the brain centers.

apraxia: inability to carry out a complex or skilled movement; not due to paralysis or impaired comprehension.

assistive technology device: equipment that is used to increase, maintain, or improve functional capabilities of a child with a disability.

asymmetric tonic reflex: a primitive reflex in which a change in body tone is triggered by the position of the head, causing an extension of one arm in the direction of the turned head, and flexion of the other, with reciprocal changes in the legs.

auditorization: the process of internally "hearing again."

auditory blending: fusion of heard parts of words into whole words.

behavior: a set relationship between a stimulus and a response.

behavior modification: a process by which a stimulus-response pattern is altered.

bilateral: working togetherness of both sides of the body.

bilateral Integration: the fine working relationship between the two sides of the body.

binocular vision: focusing, or blending into one, of the images perceived separately by the two eyes.

body image: picture or mental representation one has of one's own body, derived from internal sensation, postural changes, contact with outside objects and people, emotional experiences, and fantasies.

body schema: overall pattern of one's direct or sensory awareness of one's own body; the characteristic way in which a person is aware of his or her own body. The body image is an actual experience; the body schema is a pattern–an acquired structure that codetermines the body image in a given structure.

central visual acuity: visual faculty of perceiving the shape or form of objects in the direct line of vision.

closure (cloze): special type of assimilation, closely related to receptive functions. It involves making a "whole" from parts.

comprehension: understanding.

conceptual disorders: disturbances of thinking, reasoning, generalizing, memorizing.

contralateral: opposite side (of the body).

coordination: harmonious action of muscle groups in performing complex movements.

crossed dominance: a condition in which the preferred eye and preferred hand are on opposite sides of the body.

decoding: refers to intake of verbal symbols through auditory and/or visual pathways.

development: interaction between maturational processes and environmental influences.

directionality: projection of laterality outside the individual, which has developed inside the individual.

discrimination: the ability to differentiate between two visual, auditory, tactual, or other sensory stimuli.

dysacusis: hearing impairment which involves distortion of loudness or pitch or both, rather than loss of sensitivity.

dysarthria: articulatory disorder reflecting central nervous system dysfunction of the motor musculature of speech.

dyscalculia: inability to do simple arithmetic calculations.

dysgraphia: specific disability in which handwriting is disorganized, illegible for age/grade level.

dyskinesia: impairment of the power of voluntary movement resulting in fragmentary or incomplete movements; poor coordination.

dyslexia: inability to make sense of printed symbols; may be due to emotional, neurological, constitutional, genetic, or developmental factors.

dysrhythmia: abnormal speech fluency, usually characterized by defective stress, breath control, and intonation.

early intervention services: developmental services designed to meet the developmental needs of an infant or toddler identified by the individualized family service plan.

educational service agency: a regional public multiservice agency authorized by state law to develop, manage, and provide services or programs to local educational agencies and recognized as an administrative agency.

160

encoding: refers to output of verbal symbols through motor (speech, gestural, and/or written) pathways.

etiology: source or origin of a symptom or disease.

expressive language: generally refers to either vocal expression (speech), gestural, and/or written pathways.

eye-hand coordination: integration of the visual and tactual systems leading to the point at which the hand becomes the tool to serve the visual mechanism.

feedback: in an organism, the sensory report of the somatic result of behavior.

field of vision: entire area which can be seen without shifting the gaze.

figure-ground discrimination: ability to sort out important features, figures, characteristics.

fine motor: use of generally small muscle groups for specific, fine tasks, such as speech, oculomotor, or figure activities.

grapheme: written form of a sound unit.

imagery: the richness of detail in color, taste, smell, hearing, feeling, given to a visualization.

integration: working togetherness of the body.

intervention: most frequently, remedial treatment.

ipsilateral: same side (of the body).

kinesthesis: sensory knowledge of one's body movements.

labyrinth: part of the inner ear containing the three semi-circular canals which are concerned with position of the body in space and balance.

labyrinthine reflex: a primitive reflex triggered by the position of the head, causing either extension in the supine position or flexion in the prone position.

laterality: internal awareness of the two sides of the body and their differences.

learning: a type of behavior.

left-hemisphere: symbolic, linear, graphic, linguistic.

left-right discrimination: involves knowing the difference between left and right inside the body before projection is made outside the organism.

manifestation determination: the process of determining if a behavior resulting in a disciplinary action was a manifestation of the child's disability. The burden of proof for the manifestation determination review has now been shifted to the parents who have to prove that the behavior was caused by or had a direct and substantial relationship to the disability.

memory: recall of visual, auditory, tactile, and/or kinesthetic stimuli.

161

midline: imaginary line from tip of the head to the feet, which separates the body into halves (front view) serving as a zero point of origin.

mixed cerebral dominance: term suggesting that right or left dominance has not been completely established.

monitor: to check on or to follow progress at regular intervals.

neuromuscular re-education: training/treatment to develop a more efficient motor response to a specific stimulus.

NIMAS: (National Instructional Materials Accessibility Standard) digital files that provide an accessible representation of the printed book for blind, visually disabled, and print-disabled users

oculomotor: eye-movement behavior.

organicity: refers to the organic basis or causes of thinking and behavior difficulty or defects; suggests neurological deficits.

perception: mental interpretation of the sensations received from stimuli.

perceptual-motor problem: lack of normal functioning of either perceptual processes, motor processes, or both.

peripheral vision: peripheral or indirect vision exists when the image falls on some part of the retina outside the most sensitive part.

perseveration: continued repetition of words or motions that thus become meaningless.

phoneme: sound of a unit of writing or speech.

pronation: turning the hand or foot downward or backward.

prone: facing downward, flat.

psychomotor: relationship between the brain and the muscles.

readiness: physical, mental, and emotional preparedness for a given learning activity.

reflex: a specific motor response to a specific stimulus.

response to intervention: a procedure for identifying students with learning disabilities through the degree to which they respond to research-based instructional interventions.

rhythm: an inner awareness of time/space intervals projected through movement integration.

right-hemisphere: visual-spatial, creative, intuitive.

sensation: data a person receives through the stimulation of sensory nerve endings.

sensory-motor: relationship between sensation and movement.

sound-symbol: relationship of the sound and printed form of letters and words.

stereognosis: perception of objects or forms by touch.

symmetric tonic reflex: a change in body tone triggered by the position of the head, so that when the head is raised, the arms extend and legs flex; when the head is down, the arms flex, and legs extend.

syndrome: set of symptoms that generally occur together.

tactile: having to do with touch.

transition services: activities designed to be within a results-oriented process to facilitate the child's movement from school to post-school activities.

universal design: a concept or philosophy for designing and delivering products and services that are usable by people with the widest possible range of functional capabilities. This includes products and services that are directly usable without requiring assistive technologies and those that are made compatible with assistive technologies.

VAKT: visual-auditory-kinesthetic-tactual method of word study.

vertical imbalance: tendency of one eye to deviate upward.

verticality: feeling of "up" and "down.

vestibular stimulation: the arousal, by mechanical or physiological means, of the fluid in the inner ear (semicircular canals) affecting balance.

visual acuity: keenness of vision.

visual discrimination: adeptness at perceiving likenesses and differences in geometrical figures, pictures, and word elements.

visualization: the ability to picture, relate, and manipulate during sensory input, or following it.

visual-motor: term generally encompassing the visual receptive and motor expressive areas plus intersensory integration.

visual-perceptual problem: inability to interpret correctly what is seen.

whole-word method: word analysis without the physical separation of the word into its phonetic or structural elements.

word analysis: analysis of an unfamiliar word into known elements for the purpose of identification.

word attack skills: refers to a child's ability to analyze words by syllable and phonic elements, in order to arrive at pronunciation and meaning.

word calling: reading of words but with little or no understanding of the ideas.

Suggested Reading List

A Student's Guide to the IEP. National Dissemination Center for Children with Disabilities. January 2002. www.nichcy.org/pubs/stguide/st1book.htm (2006).

Avoiding an IEP Disaster. Parts 1–6. (video, producer unknown). Baltimore: National Association of Parents of Blind Children, 1998.

Bateman, Barbara D. and Herr, Cynthia M. *Writing Measurable IEP Goals and Objectives.* Attainment Company Inc., 2006

Bennett, T., C. Zhang, and L. Hojnar. "Facilitating the Full Participation of Culturally Diverse Families in the IEP Process." *Infant-Toddler Intervention: The Transdisciplinary Journal,* 8 (3), 227–249, 1998.

Bigge, J. L. and C. S. Stump. *Curriculum, Assessment and Instruction for Students with Disabilities.* Wadsworth Special Educator Series. Belmont, CA: Wadsworth Publishing Co., 1999.

Espin, Christine A., Stanley L. Deno, and Deniz Albayrak-Kaymak. "Individualized Education Programs in Resource and Inclusive Settings: How 'Individualized' Are They?" *Journal of Special Education,* 32 (3), 164–174, Fall 1998.

Families and Advocates Partnership for Education. *IDEA 2004 Summary.* n.d. www.fape.org/idea/2004/summary.htm (2006).

Hayes, Marnell L. *The Turned-In, Turned-on Book about Learning Problems.* Revised. Novato, CA: Academic Therapy Publications, 1994.

Knoblauch, Bernadette and Kathleen McLane. *An Overview of the Individuals with Disabilities Education Act Amendments of 1997* (P.L. 105-17): Update 1999. June 1999. Education Resources Information Center. ERIC Identifier: ED433668.

Learning Disabilities Association of America. *LDA Recommendations on IDEA Regulations.* February 2005. www.ldaamerica.org/legislative/bulletins/recommend.asp (July 2006).

Lillie, T. "What Research Says about Communicating with Parents of Children with

Disabilities and What Teachers Should Know." Paper presented at the 46th Annual Convention of the Ohio Federation Council of Exceptional Children, November 1998.

"Linkage of IEP to the General Education Curriculum." (forum) National Association of State Directors of Special Education, Alexandria, VA, 1999.

Osman, Betty S. with Henriette L. Blinder. *No One to Play With: social problems of LD and ADD children.* Novato, CA: Academic Therapy Publications, 1995.

Pruitt, P., et al. "Listen to Us! Parents Speak Out about Interactions with Special Educators." Preventing School Failure, 42 (4), 161–166, Summer 1998.

Rebhorn, Theresa. *Developing Your Child's IEP.* National Dissemination Center for Children with Disabilities. October, 2002. www.nichcy.org/pubs/parent/pa12txt.htm (2006).

School, Beverly and Arlene Cooper. *The IEP Primer and the Individualized Program.* Novato, CA: Academic Therapy Publications, 1999.

Steedman, Wayne. *10 Tips: how to use IDEA 2004 to improve your child's special education.* 2005. www.wrightslaw.com/idea/art/10.tips.steedman.htm (2006).

Warger, Cynthia. "New IDEA '97 Requirements: Factors to Consider in Developing an IEP." August 1999. Education Resources Information Center. ERIC Identifier: ED434434.

Wisconsin State Department of Public Instruction. *A Parent's Guide to Transition for Youth with Disabilities.* Madison, WI, 1998.